HELLO,
my name is:

And I'm a Cat Lady

YASMINE SUROVEC

A *creative* journal for Cat Lovers

Andrews McMeel
PUBLISHING®

This Journal Belongs To:

How to use this journal

This journal is for documenting the day-to-day nuances and quirks of a cat person and his/her cat.

There is no right or wrong way to answer each prompt in the journal. You can draw, add photos, make a collage, or simply write your answers down. This is about you, and your cat, and the life you've built around one another. Make it yours!

Oh, and if you see a blank, dotted line in the title of each entry, write down your cat's name.

Anyway, I hope you have fun completing this journal as much as I've enjoyed creating it for you!

Your friendly neighborhood cat lady,
Yasmine

The Story of US

Tell the story of how you and your
BEST FRIEND came into each
other's lives

When did you meet?

How did you meet?

What was your first thought/reaction?

What was his/her first reaction?

Did you take her/him home immediately?

Do you have other furry (and non-furry)
friends at home? How did they react?

Did you take him/her to the vet?

- -

- -

Did it take long before she/he acclimated to
her/his new home?

- -

- -

Did she/he warm up to you easily? Or did it take
some time?

- -

- -

If and when (s)he warmed up to you, what was
the first thing (s)he did?

- -

- -

Once (s)he warmed up to you, how did you feel?

- -

- -

Describe your most favorite part
of having her/him in your life.

- -

- -

Your current mood

- ◯ HAPPY
- ◯ SAD
- ◯ ECSTATIC
- ◯ DEPRESSED
- ◯ INDIFFERENT
- ◯ APATHETIC

- ◯ EXCITED
- ◯ BORED
- ◯ SLEEPY
- ◯ ENERGETIC
- ◯ TIRED
- ◯ ANGRY

- ◯ HUNGRY
- ◯ FULL
- ◯ SILLY
- ◯ BUSY
- ◯ GRUMPY
- ◯ OPTIMISTIC

◯ _ _ _ _ _ _ _ _ _ _ _ _

ADD FACE (AND HAIR)

_ _ _ _ _ _ _ _'s current mood

- ◯ CRAZY
- ◯ CONTENT
- ◯ KINDA MEH
- ◯ SLEEPY
- ◯ HUNGRY
- ◯ STALKER-Y

- ◯ AFFECTIONATE
- ◯ ENERGETIC
- ◯ JUMPY
- ◯ PLAYFUL
- ◯ FRIGHTENED
- ◯ ANGRY

- ◯ HAPPY
- ◯ ALERT
- ◯ FRANTIC
- ◯ RELAXED
- ◯ DEPRESSED
- ◯ EXCITED

◯ _ _ _ _ _ _ _ _ _ _ _ _

ADD FACE (AND MARKINGS)

DATE: _ _ _ _ _ _ _ _ _ _ _

YOU ARE THE JANE GOODALL OF THE DOMESTICATED CAT WORLD

What is the cat doing at this moment?

☐ sleeping

☐ demanding to be fed

☐ staring at the wall

☐ puking hairballs

☐ hunting

☐ cuddling with me

☐ avoiding me

☐ destroying something

☐ being playful

☐ I have absolutely no clue where (s)he is at this time

☐ looking down on me

☐ shedding on my clothes

☐ running around

☐ _ _ _ _ _ _ _ _ _ _ _ _ _ _ _ _

☐ _ _ _ _ _ _ _ _ _ _ _ _ _ _ _ _

ADD YOUR OBSERVATIONS

15 QUESTIONS _____ WOULD LIKELY ASK YOU

1.

2.

3.

4.

5.

6.

7.

8.

9.

10.

11.

12.

13.

14.

15.

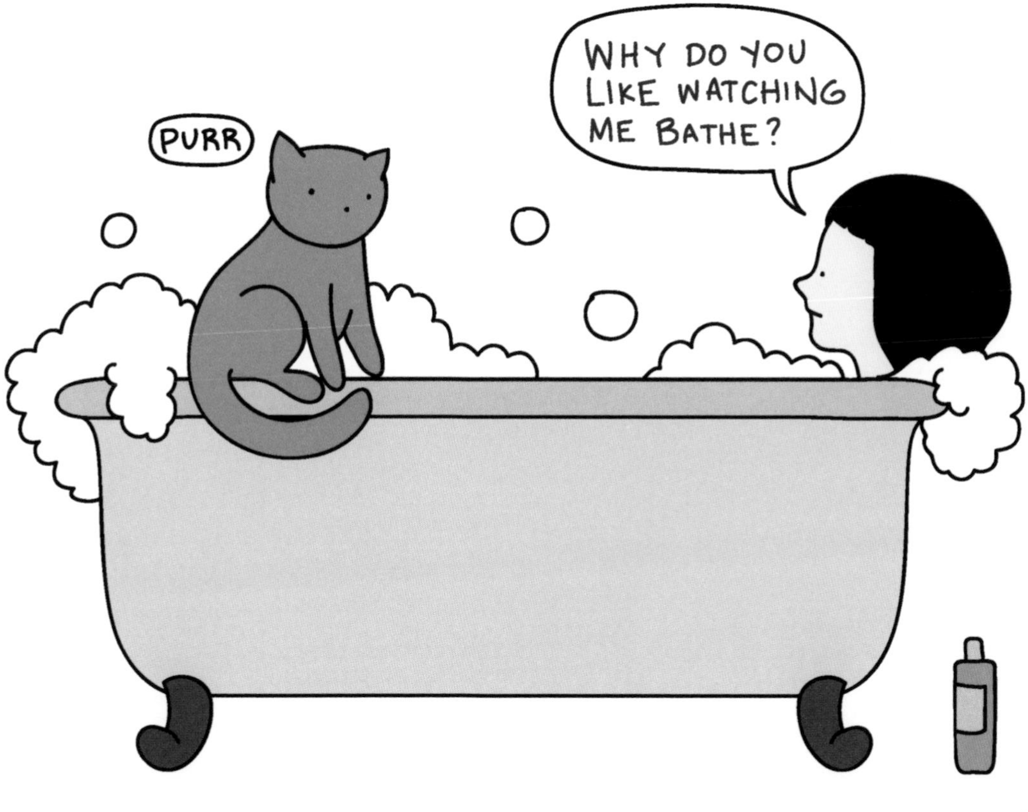
PURR
WHY DO YOU LIKE WATCHING ME BATHE?

A DAY IN THE LIFE OF A HUMAN

12AM _____

_____

1AM _____

_____

2AM _____

_____

3AM _____

_____

4AM _____

_____

5AM _____

_____

6AM _____

_____

7AM _____

_____

8AM _____

_____

9AM _____

_____

10AM _____

_____

11AM _____

_____

12PM _____

_____

1PM _____

_____

2PM _____

_____

3PM _____

_____

4PM _____

_____

5PM _____

_____

6PM _____

_____

7PM _____

_____

8PM _____

_____

9PM _____

_____

10PM _____

_____

11PM _____

_____

12AM _____

_____

Miscellaneous notes

A DAY IN THE LIFE OF A CAT

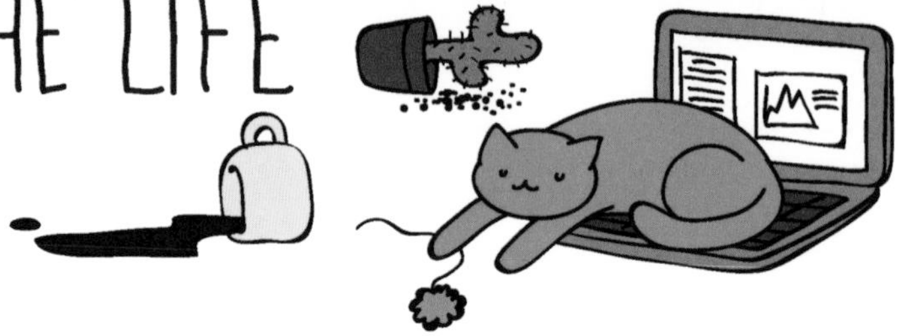

12AM

1AM

2AM

3AM

4AM

5AM

6AM

7AM

8AM

9AM

10AM

11AM

12PM

1PM

2PM --------------------------------

3PM --------------------------------

4PM --------------------------------

5PM --------------------------------

6PM --------------------------------

7PM --------------------------------

8PM --------------------------------

9PM --------------------------------

10PM --------------------------------

11PM --------------------------------

12AM --------------------------------

Miscellaneous notes

20 REASONS WHY I'M *grateful* FOR --------------------

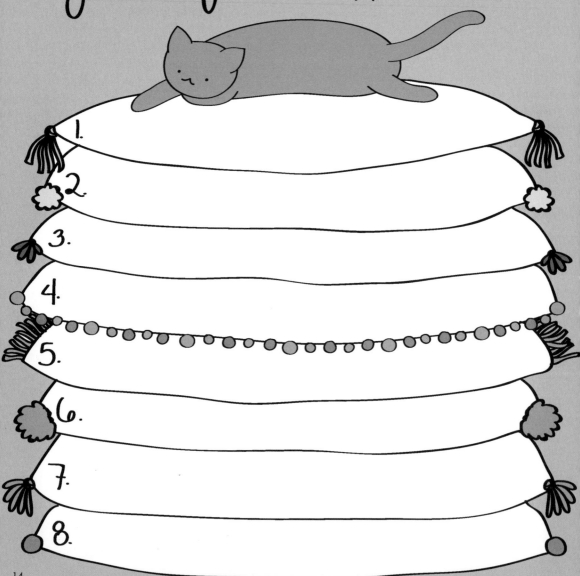

1.
2.
3.
4.
5.
6.
7.
8.

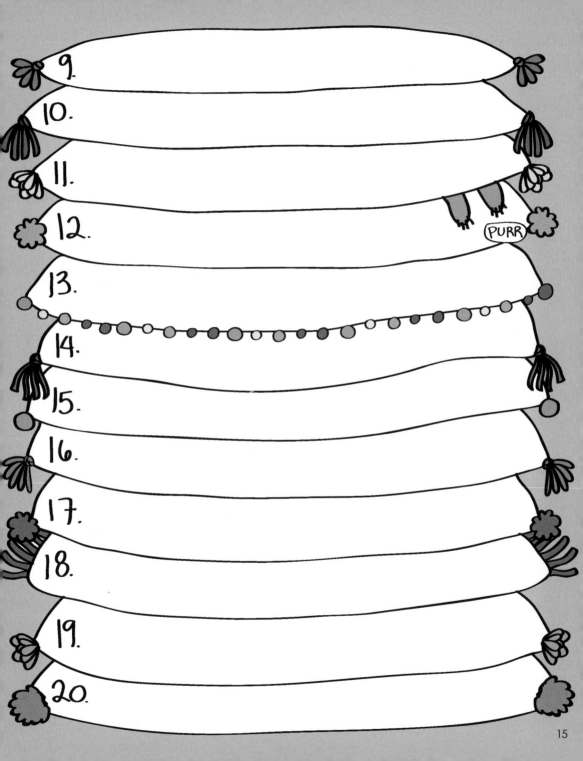

9.

10.

11.

12.   PURR

13.

14.

15.

16.

17.

18.

19.

20.

If you were to give advice
to .... , what would it be?

RANDOM THOUGHT OF THE DAY

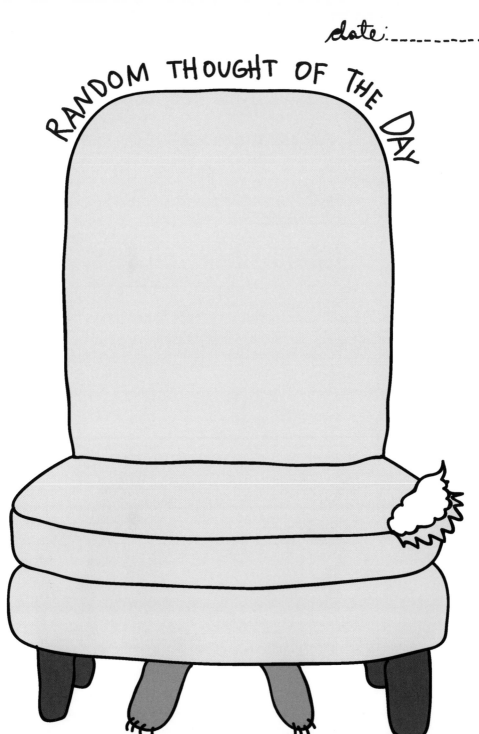

17

Are there other cat persons in your life?

DESCRIBE HIM OR HER.

DOES _____ LET YOU TOUCH HIS/HER BELLY?

IF YES, DOES IT FEEL LIKE TOUCHING THE MOST MAGICAL, FLUFFY THING ON EARTH?

CAT BADGES

Cross out the badge(s) your cat wins today

SPILLED BEVERAGE

UNEATEN
CAT FOOD

LITTER BOX
SLUMBER

FURRY WARDROBE

CARDBOARD BOX
ENTHUSIAST

CRITTER EATER

HIDE AND SEEK
EXPERT

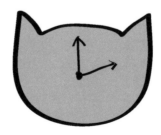

ALARM CLOCK

STRESS
RELIEVER

LAP WARMER

HOME
PROTECTOR

BATH TIME
COMPANION

FOOD THIEF

RANDOM THING
HOARDER

STEALTHY
SWIPER

WALL STARER

BACK MASSAGER

A SHOULDER
TO CRY ON

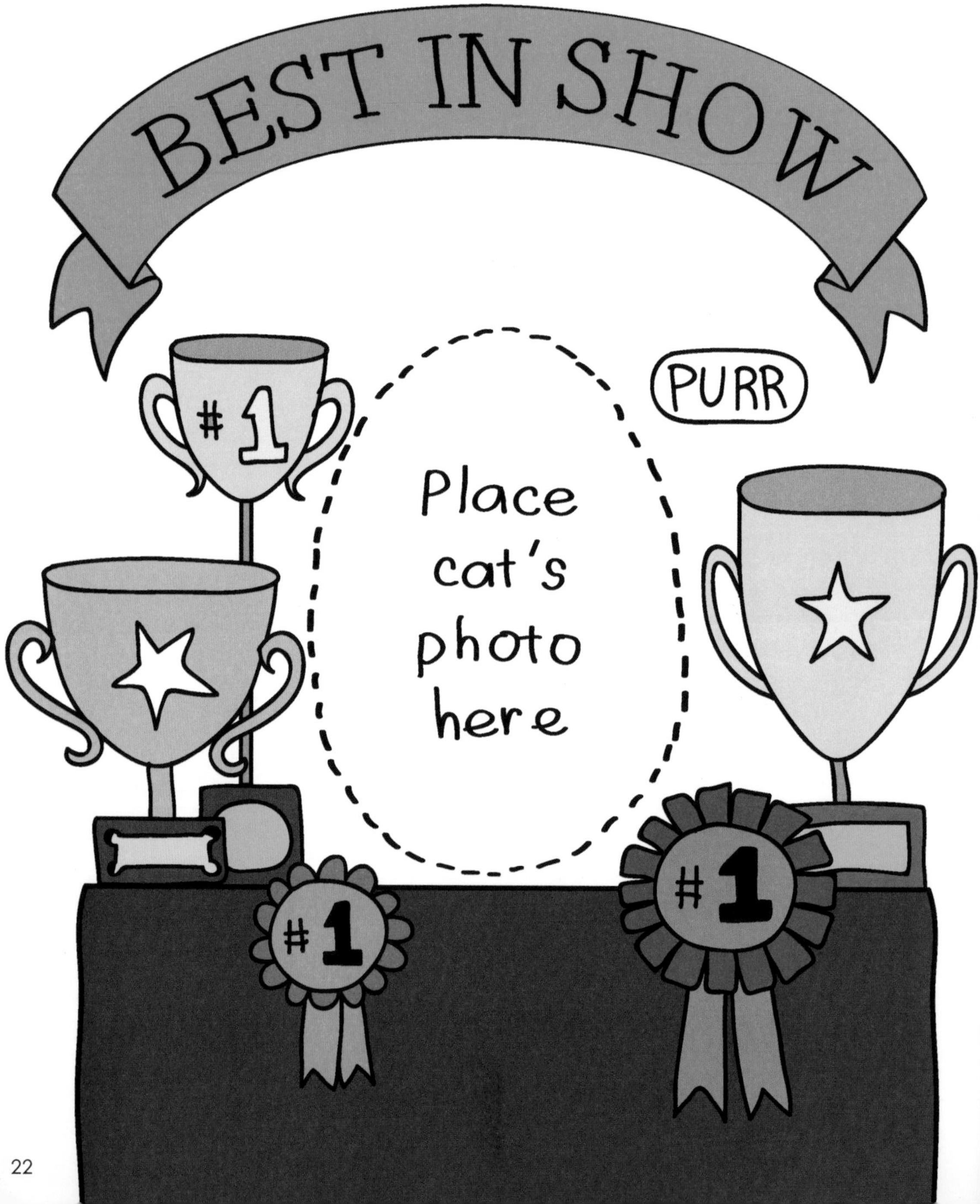
BEST IN SHOW
#1
PURR
Place
cat's
photo
here
#1
#1

THE CAT HAS BEEN STARING AT A BLANK WALL
FOR THE LONGEST TIME.
WHAT COULD (S)HE BE POSSIBLY BE SEEING?

Your current mood

- ◯ HAPPY
- ◯ SAD
- ◯ ECSTATIC
- ◯ DEPRESSED
- ◯ INDIFFERENT
- ◯ APATHETIC

- ◯ EXCITED
- ◯ BORED
- ◯ SLEEPY
- ◯ ENERGETIC
- ◯ TIRED
- ◯ ANGRY

- ◯ HUNGRY
- ◯ FULL
- ◯ SILLY
- ◯ BUSY
- ◯ GRUMPY
- ◯ OPTIMISTIC

◯ _ _ _ _ _ _ _ _ _ _ _ _ _ _

ADD FACE (AND HAIR)

_ _ _ _ _ _ _ _'s current mood

- ◯ CRAZY
- ◯ CONTENT
- ◯ KINDA MEH
- ◯ SLEEPY
- ◯ HUNGRY
- ◯ STALKER-Y

- ◯ AFFECTIONATE
- ◯ ENERGETIC
- ◯ JUMPY
- ◯ PLAYFUL
- ◯ FRIGHTENED
- ◯ ANGRY

- ◯ HAPPY
- ◯ ALERT
- ◯ FRANTIC
- ◯ RELAXED
- ◯ DEPRESSED
- ◯ EXCITED

◯ _ _ _ _ _ _ _ _ _ _ _ _ _ _

ADD FACE (AND MARKINGS)

DATE: _ _ _ _ _ _ _ _ _ _ _

YOU ARE THE JANE GOODALL
OF THE DOMESTICATED
CAT WORLD

What is the cat doing at this moment?

☐ sleeping

☐ demanding to be fed

☐ staring at the wall

☐ puking hairballs

☐ hunting

☐ cuddling with me

☐ avoiding me

☐ destroying something

☐ being playful

☐ I have absolutely no clue where (s)he is at this time

☐ looking down on me

☐ shedding on my clothes

☐ running around

☐ _____

☐ _____

ADD YOUR OBSERVATIONS

YAY! It's ....'s Birthday!

YOU'RE GOING TO BE THE PARTY PLANNER

DESCRIBE THE THEME

MAKE A LIST OF SUPPLIES

WHAT'S ON THE MENU?

WHO'S INVITED?

DRAW THE FANCIEST BIRTHDAY CAKE YET!

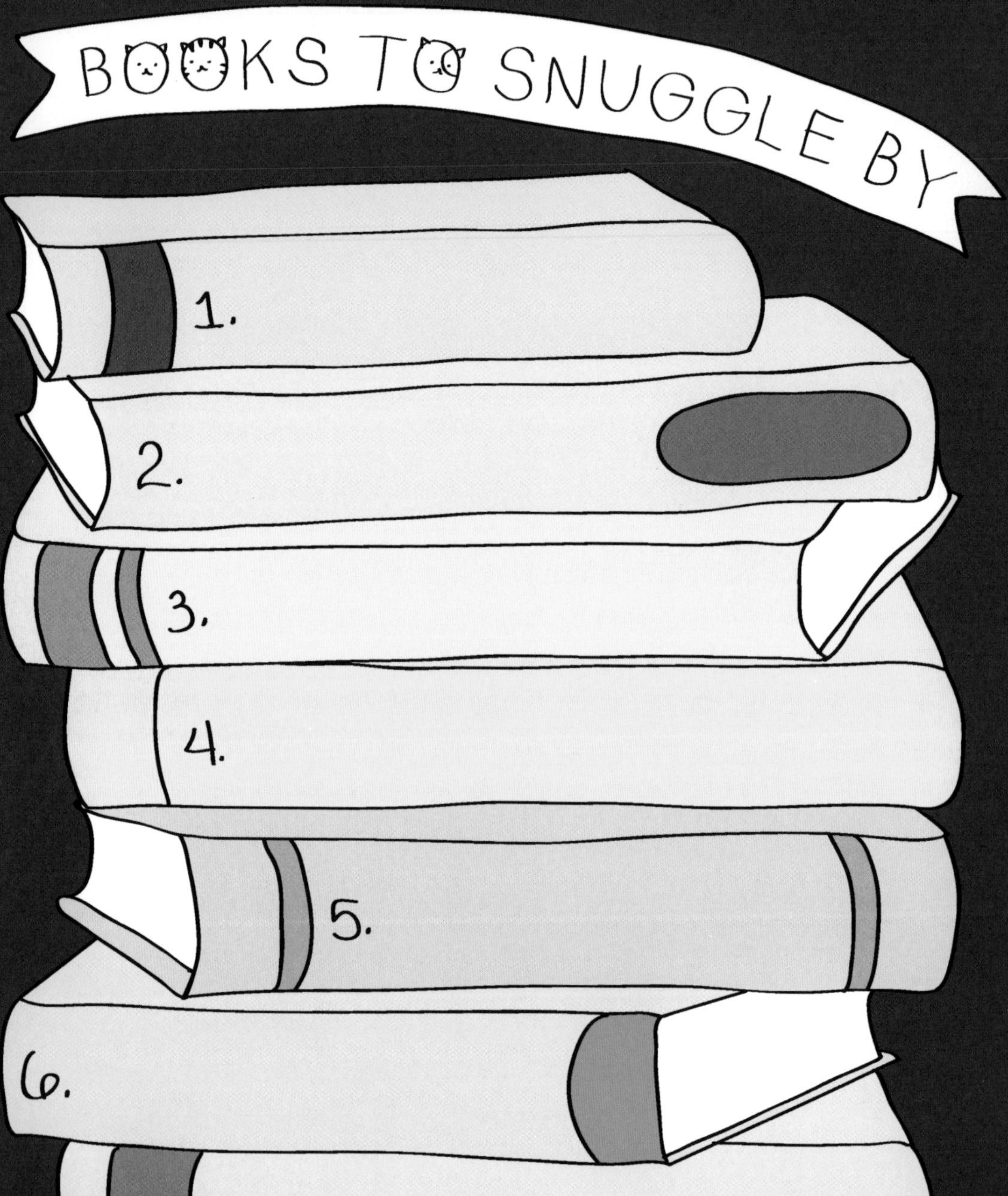
BOOKS TO SNUGGLE BY
1.
2.
3.
4.
5.
6.
7.

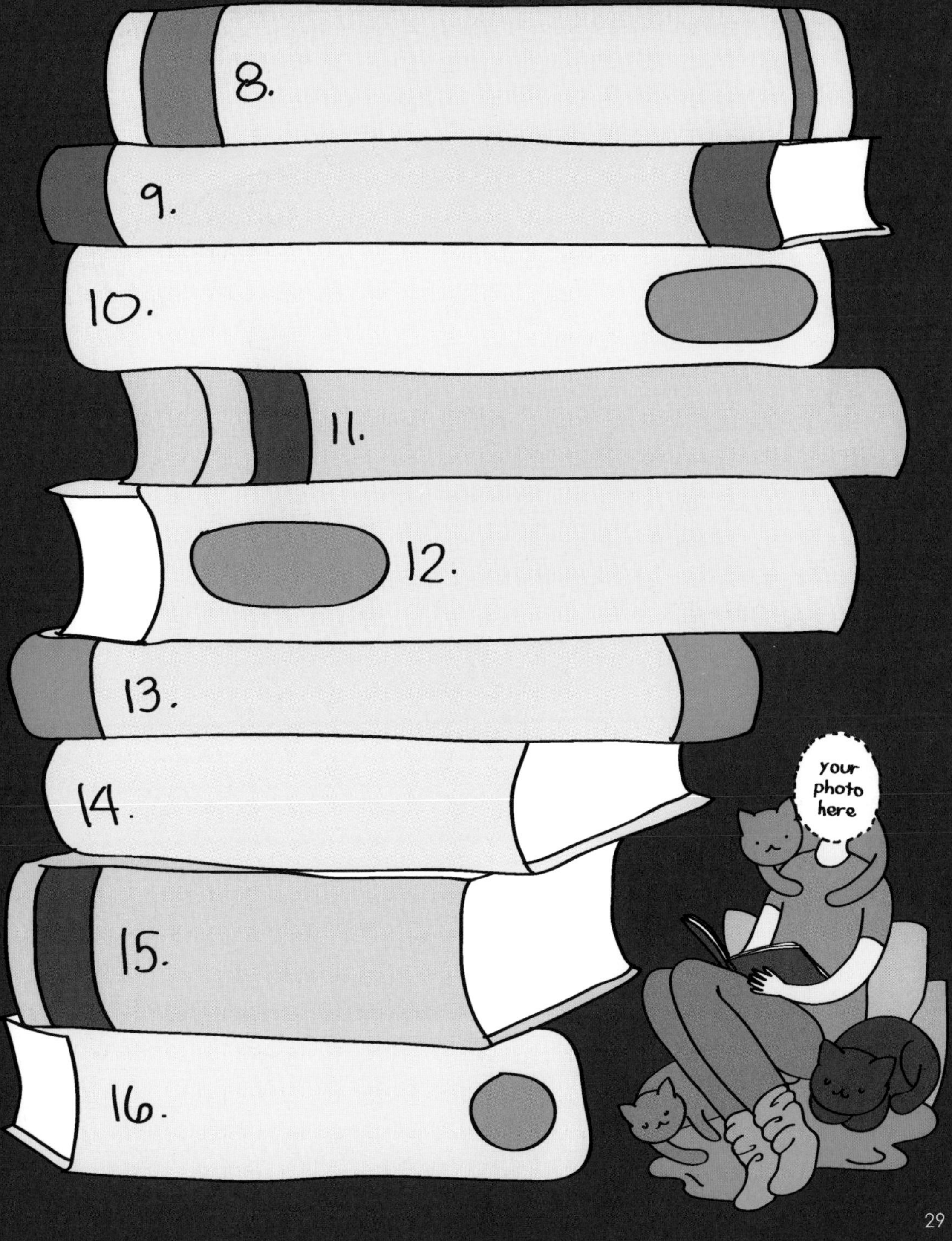
8.
9.
10.
11.
12.
13.
14.
15.
16.
your photo here

Boop this page

RANDOM THOUGHT of the DAY

WHEN WAS THE LAST STRESSFUL TIME

_____ WAS THERE FOR YOU?

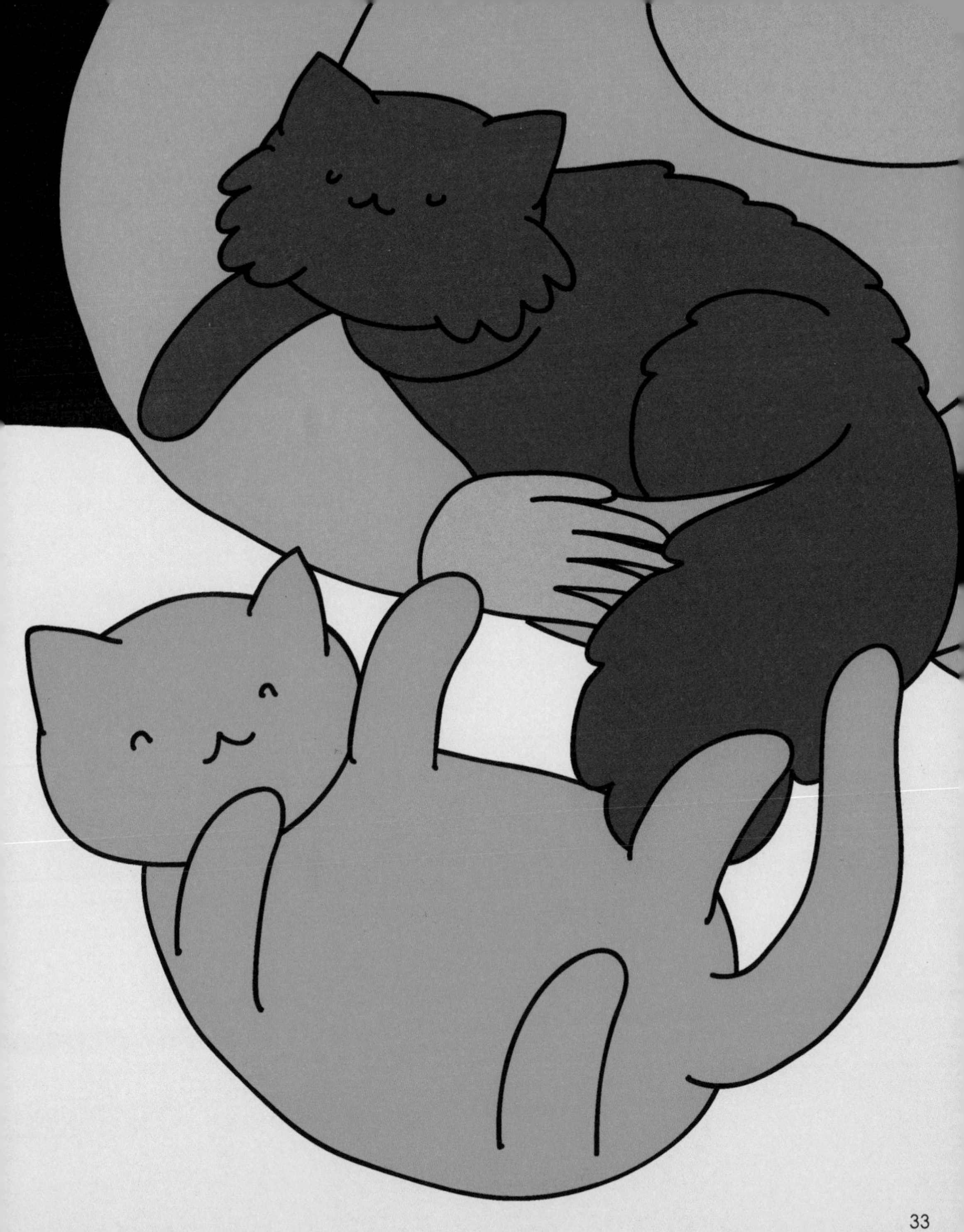

You run your very own
CAT CAFE

name:

menu for humans

menu for cats

types of furniture and decor

cat accessories

music

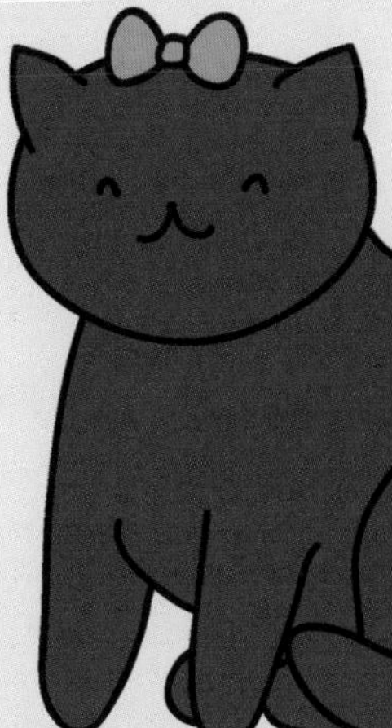

Make a list of your FELINE-loving friends

1.

2.

3.

4.

5.

6.

7.

8.

9.

10.

11.

12.

DON'T HAVE ANY HUMAN FRIENDS?
THAT'S OKAY. THAT'S WHAT OUR FURRY
(AND FEATHERY, SCALY, AND, UM,
SLIMY) FRIENDS ARE FOR!

WHAT IS YOUR HOME LIKE?

COLOR THIS PAGE

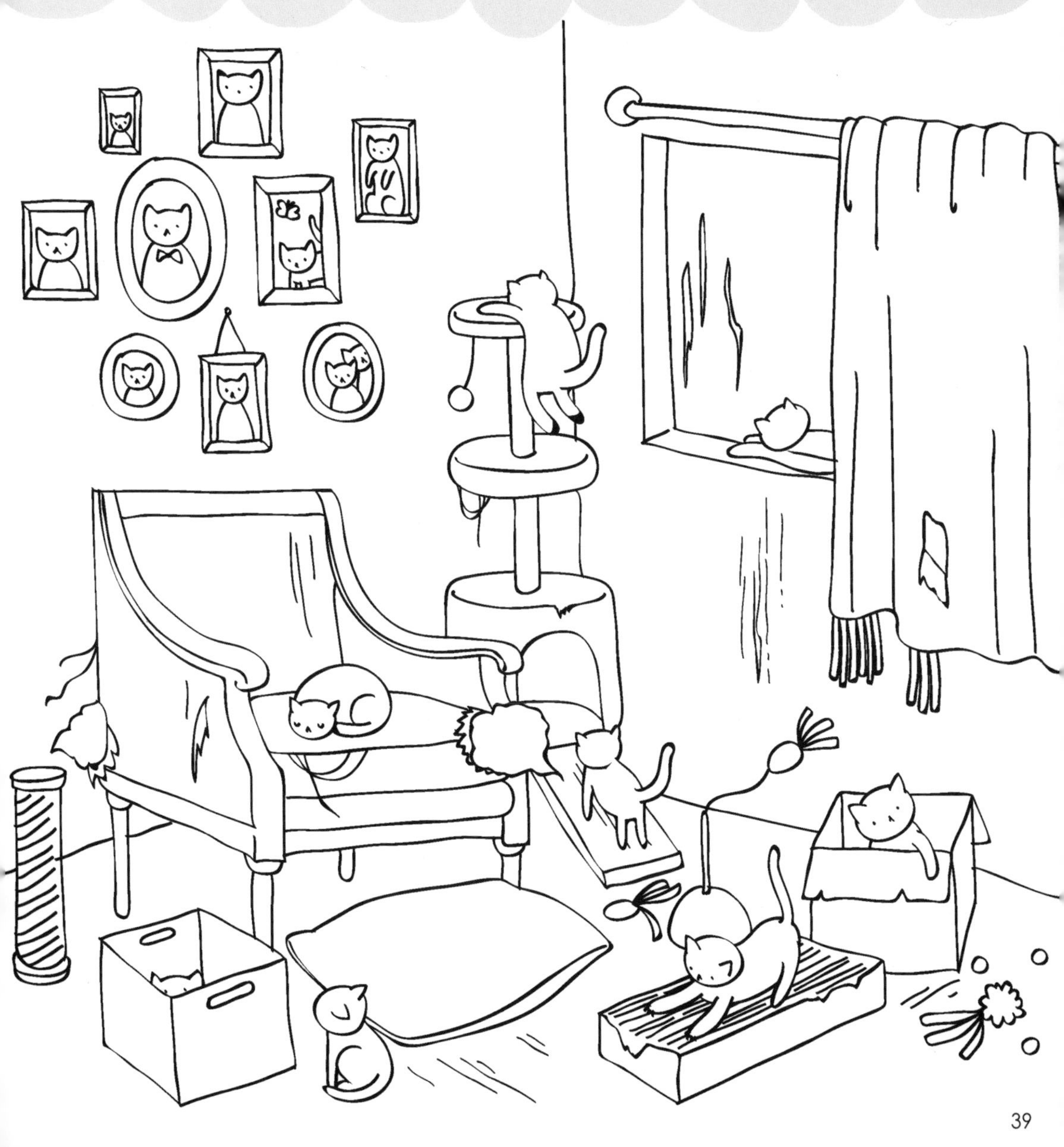

SLEEPING POSITION DOODLES

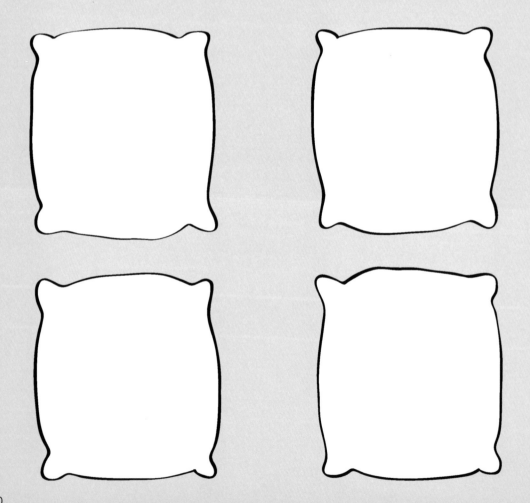

Your current mood

- ⃝ HAPPY
- ⃝ SAD
- ⃝ ECSTATIC
- ⃝ DEPRESSED
- ⃝ INDIFFERENT
- ⃝ APATHETIC

- ⃝ EXCITED
- ⃝ BORED
- ⃝ SLEEPY
- ⃝ ENERGETIC
- ⃝ TIRED
- ⃝ ANGRY

- ⃝ HUNGRY
- ⃝ FULL
- ⃝ SILLY
- ⃝ BUSY
- ⃝ GRUMPY
- ⃝ OPTIMISTIC

⃝ _ _ _ _ _ _ _ _ _ _ _

ADD FACE (AND HAIR)

_ _ _ _ _ _ _ 's current mood

- ⃝ CRAZY
- ⃝ CONTENT
- ⃝ KINDA MEH
- ⃝ SLEEPY
- ⃝ HUNGRY
- ⃝ STALKER-Y

- ⃝ AFFECTIONATE
- ⃝ ENERGETIC
- ⃝ JUMPY
- ⃝ PLAYFUL
- ⃝ FRIGHTENED
- ⃝ ANGRY

- ⃝ HAPPY
- ⃝ ALERT
- ⃝ FRANTIC
- ⃝ RELAXED
- ⃝ DEPRESSED
- ⃝ EXCITED

⃝ _ _ _ _ _ _ _ _ _ _ _

ADD FACE (AND MARKINGS)

DATE: _ _ _ _ _ _ _ _ _ _

YOU ARE THE JANE GOODALL OF THE DOMESTICATED CAT WORLD

What is the cat doing at this moment?

- [ ] sleeping
- [ ] demanding to be fed
- [ ] staring at the wall
- [ ] puking hairballs
- [ ] hunting
- [ ] cuddling with me
- [ ] avoiding me
- [ ] destroying something
- [ ] being playful
- [ ] I have absolutely no clue where (s)he is at this time
- [ ] looking down on me
- [ ] shedding on my clothes
- [ ] running around
- [ ] _
- [ ] _

ADD YOUR OBSERVATIONS

43

LIST FOR THE CAT SITTER

44

ADDITIONAL NOTES

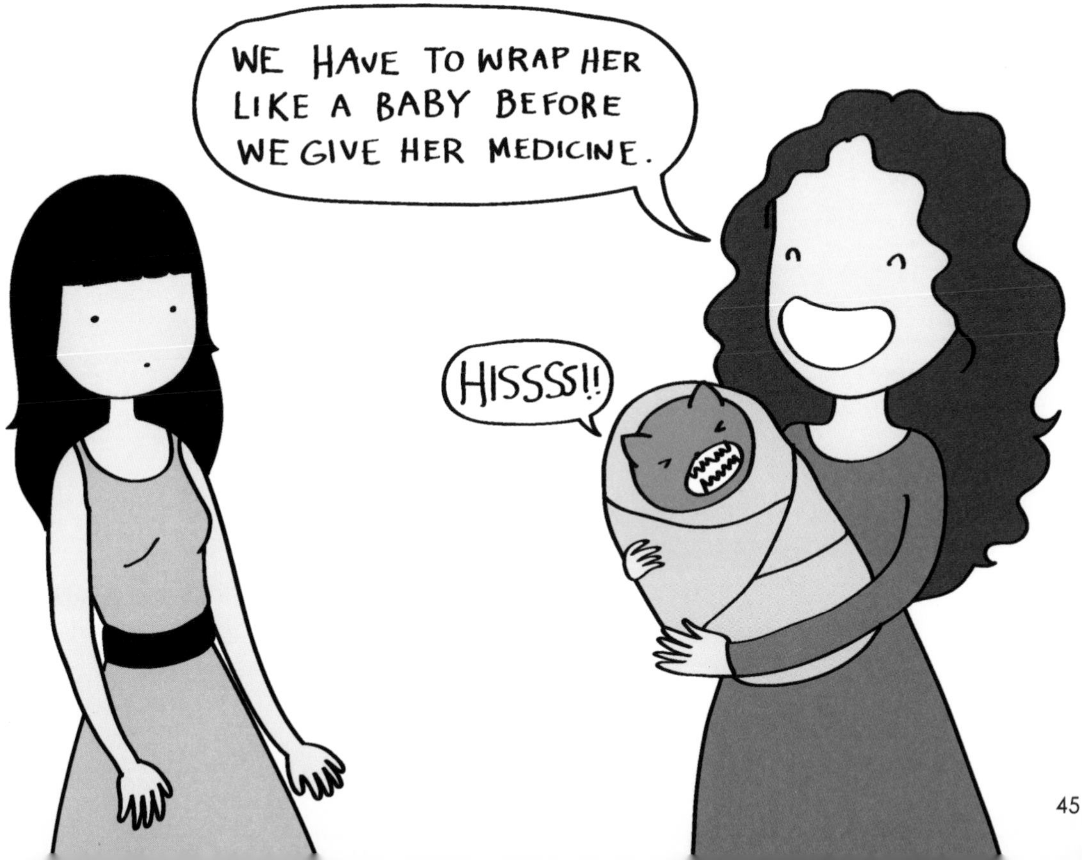
WE HAVE TO WRAP HER LIKE A BABY BEFORE WE GIVE HER MEDICINE.
HISSSS!!

DESIGN THE MOST *amazing*, MOST *awesome*, MOST *fantastical* CAT TOWER YET!

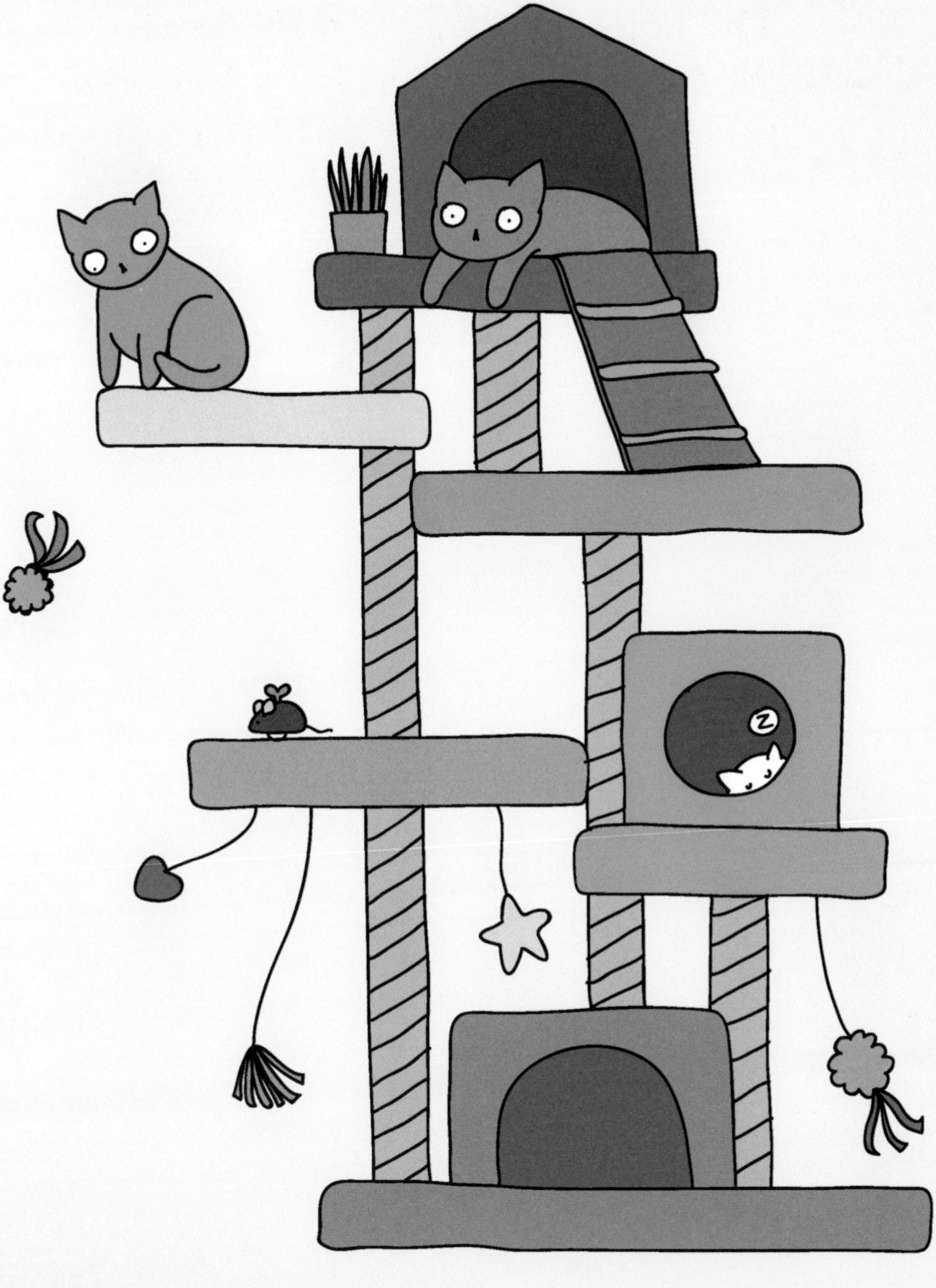
z

THAT WAS FUN! NOW DESIGN
THE MOST *amazing*, MOST *awesome*,
MOST *fantastical* CAT TOY!

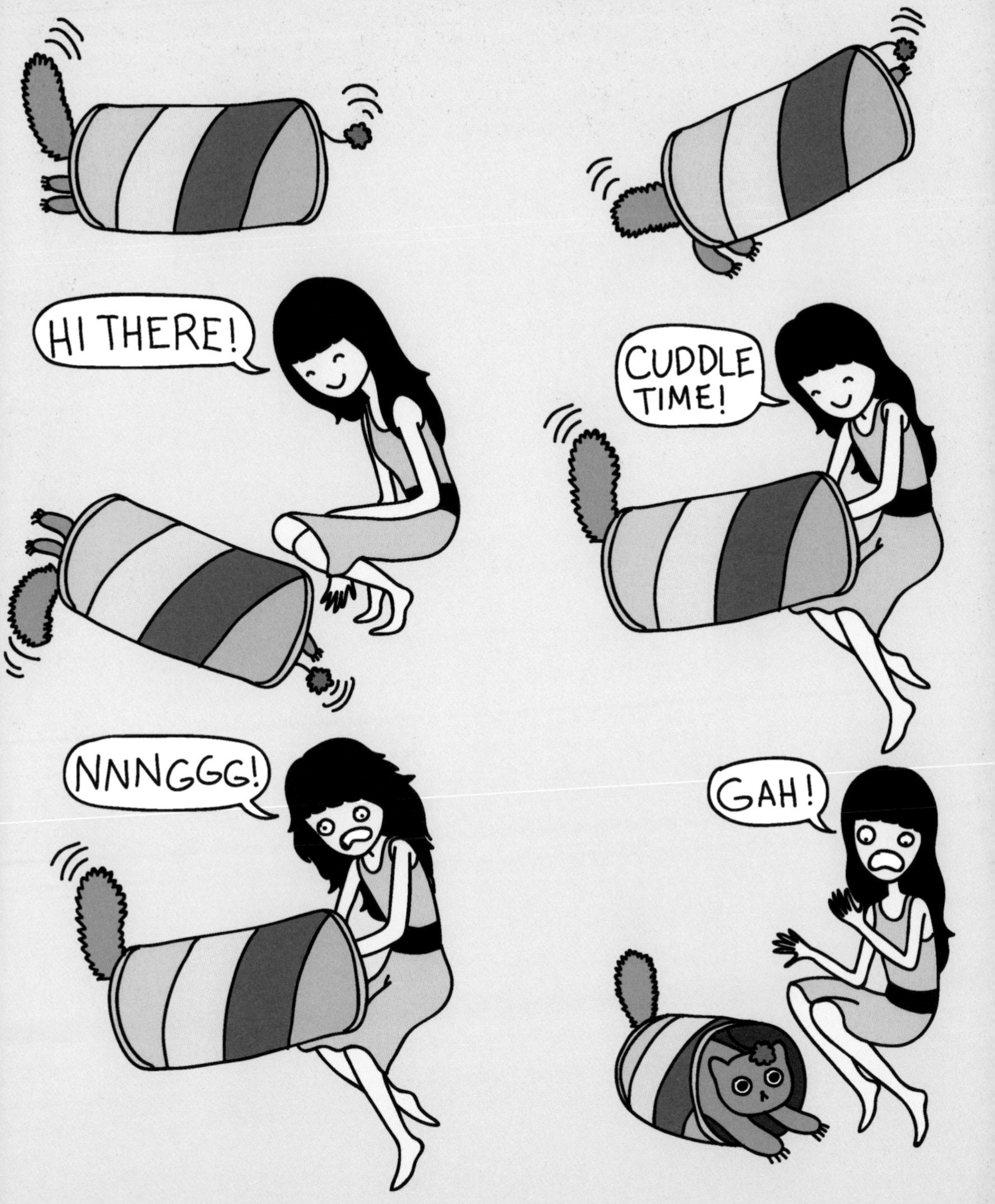
HI THERE!
CUDDLE TIME!
NNNGGG!
GAH!

What part of your bed does your cat(s) like to hang out in?

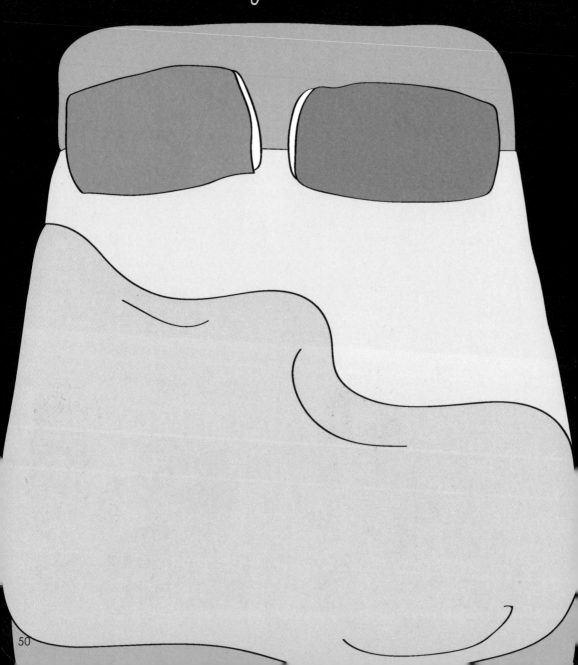

Random thought of the Day

TAKE A LONG NAP.
YOU DESERVE IT!

Sprinkle some catnip on this page, and let your cat roll all over it

CATS >

_____
_____
_____
_____
_____
_____
_____
_____
_____
_____
_____
_____
_____
_____
_____

Aside from cats,
what other animals do you love?

THINGS CATS EAT BUT SHOULDN'T

Cross out the items your cat has eaten

PURR

NOM

DRAW OR CREATE A LIST OF THINGS
YOUR CAT LIKES TO EAT

WHAT ARE _____'S FAVORITES?

Cat food:

Treats:

Litter:

Thing to play with:

Human:

Thing to do during the day:

Thing to do at night:

Thing to do when the human isn't home:

Thing to do outside the house (if allowed):

Place to nap on:

Thing to climb on:

Your current mood

- ◯ HAPPY
- ◯ SAD
- ◯ ECSTATIC
- ◯ DEPRESSED
- ◯ INDIFFERENT
- ◯ APATHETIC

- ◯ EXCITED
- ◯ BORED
- ◯ SLEEPY
- ◯ ENERGETIC
- ◯ TIRED
- ◯ ANGRY

- ◯ HUNGRY
- ◯ FULL
- ◯ SILLY
- ◯ BUSY
- ◯ GRUMPY
- ◯ OPTIMISTIC

- ◯ _____

ADD FACE (AND HAIR)

_____'s current mood

- ◯ CRAZY
- ◯ CONTENT
- ◯ KINDA MEH
- ◯ SLEEPY
- ◯ HUNGRY
- ◯ STALKER-Y

- ◯ AFFECTIONATE
- ◯ ENERGETIC
- ◯ JUMPY
- ◯ PLAYFUL
- ◯ FRIGHTENED
- ◯ ANGRY

- ◯ HAPPY
- ◯ ALERT
- ◯ FRANTIC
- ◯ RELAXED
- ◯ DEPRESSED
- ◯ EXCITED

- ◯ _____

ADD FACE (AND MARKINGS)

DATE: _____

60

YOU ARE THE JANE GOODALL OF THE DOMESTICATED CAT WORLD

What is the cat doing at this moment?

- ☐ sleeping
- ☐ demanding to be fed
- ☐ staring at the wall
- ☐ puking hairballs
- ☐ hunting
- ☐ cuddling with me
- ☐ avoiding me
- ☐ destroying something
- ☐ being playful
- ☐ I have absolutely no clue where (s)he is at this time
- ☐ looking down on me
- ☐ shedding on my clothes
- ☐ running around
- ☐ _
- ☐ _

ADD YOUR OBSERVATIONS

Gallery of Cats

FROM THE PAST

Ways................gives you comfort
during stressful times:

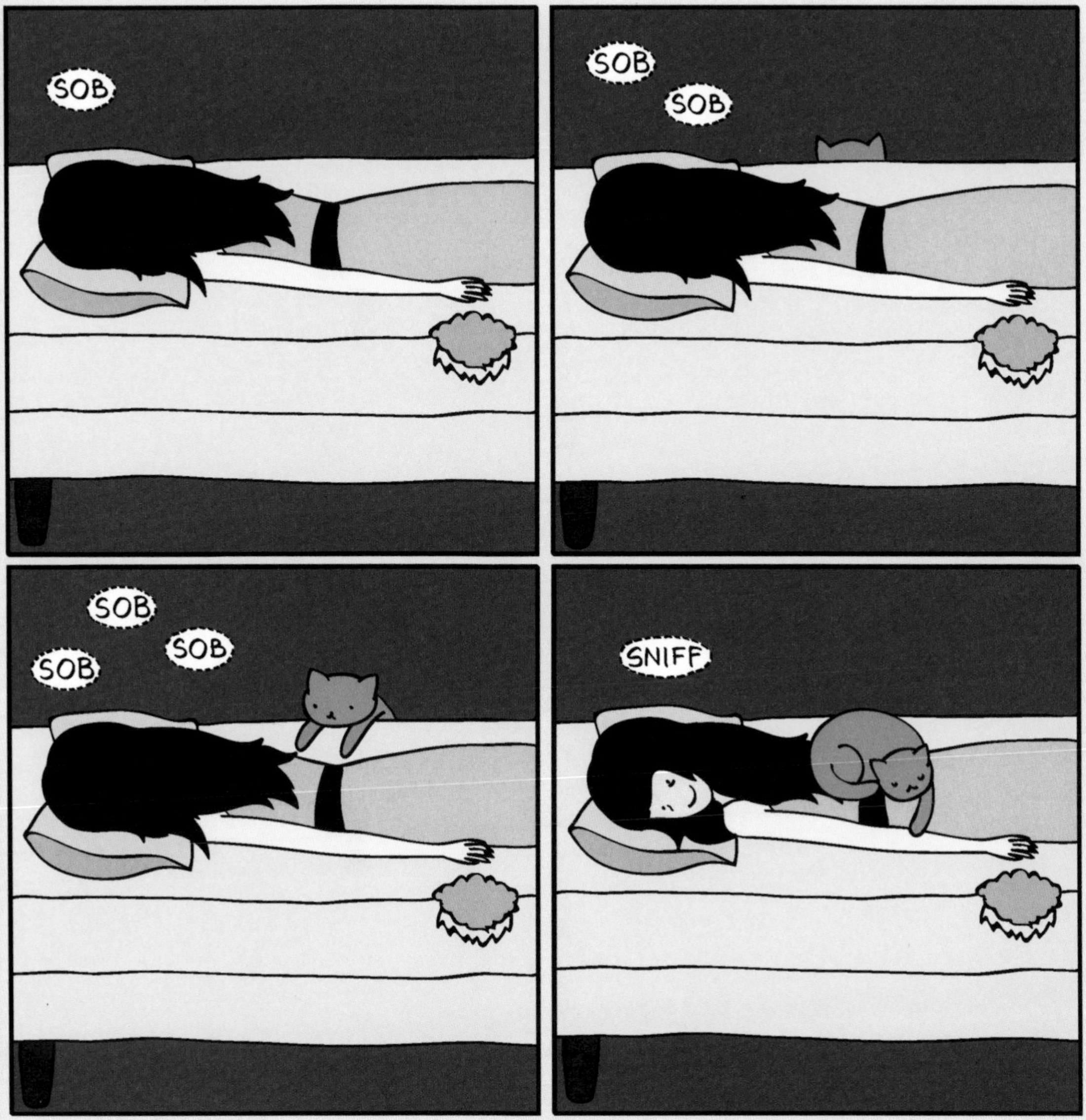
SOB
SOB
SOB
SOB
SOB
SOB
SNIFF

Draw your couch, er, your cat's couch

WHAT KIND OF CAT LADY ARE YOU?

- fabulous
- amazing
- sexy
- super awesome
- joyful
- energetic
- the best
- _____

You will receive much joy in the company of felines

Random Thought of the Day

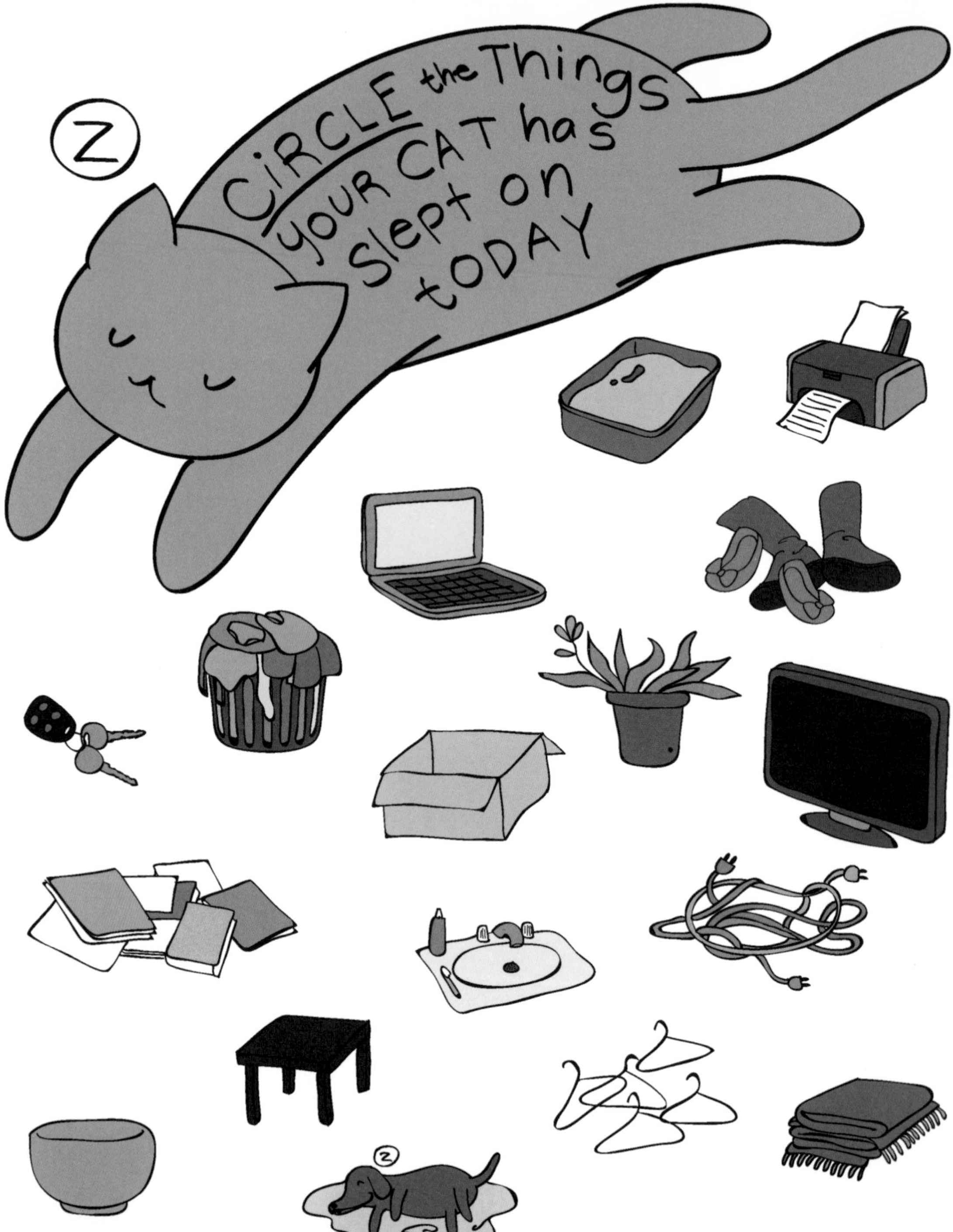
CIRCLE the Things your CAT has Slept on TODAY

DRAW OR CREATE A LIST OF THINGS THE CAT LIKES TO SLEEP ON BUT SHOULDN'T

TIME FOR
A CUDDLE
BREAK!

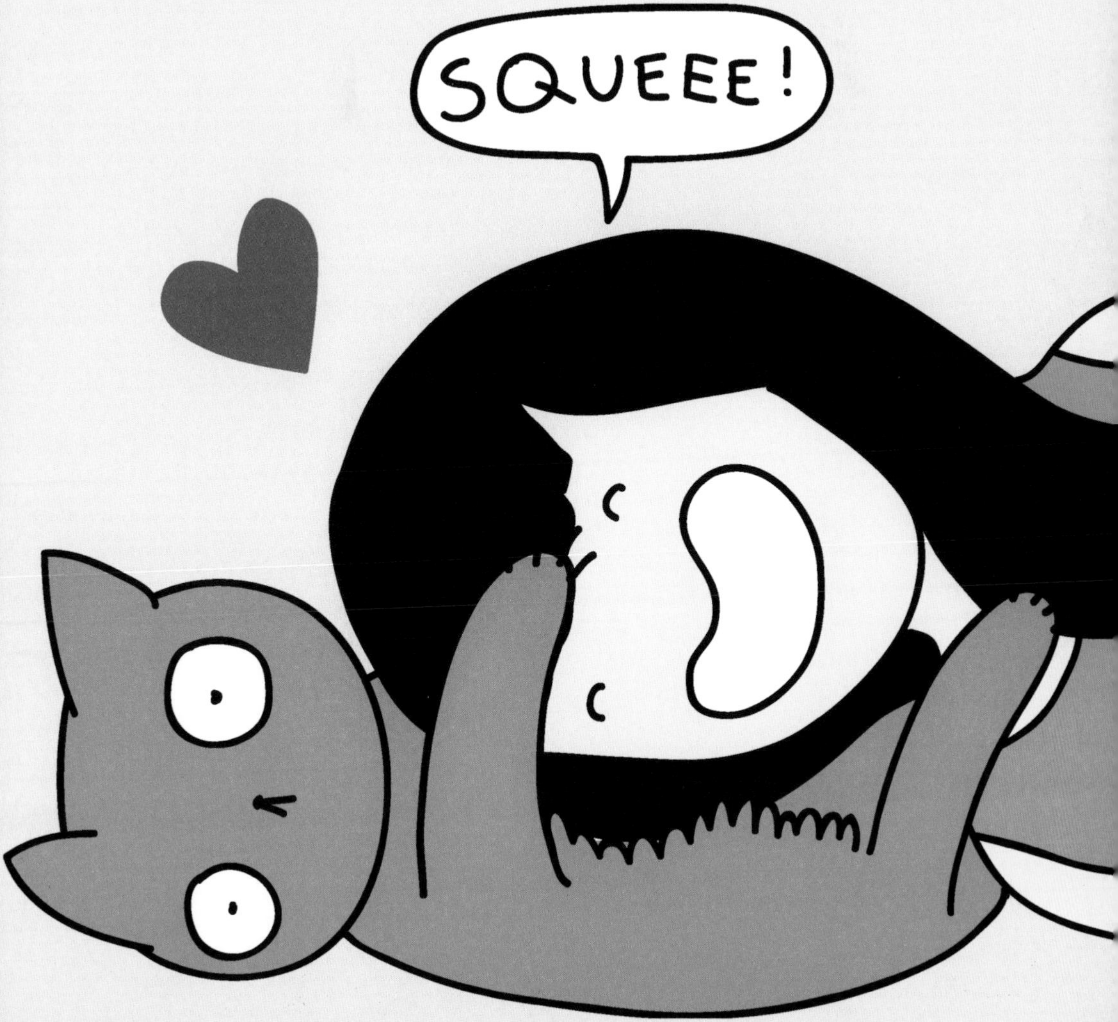
SQUEEE!

Have you ever dreamt about cats?
Describe those dreams.

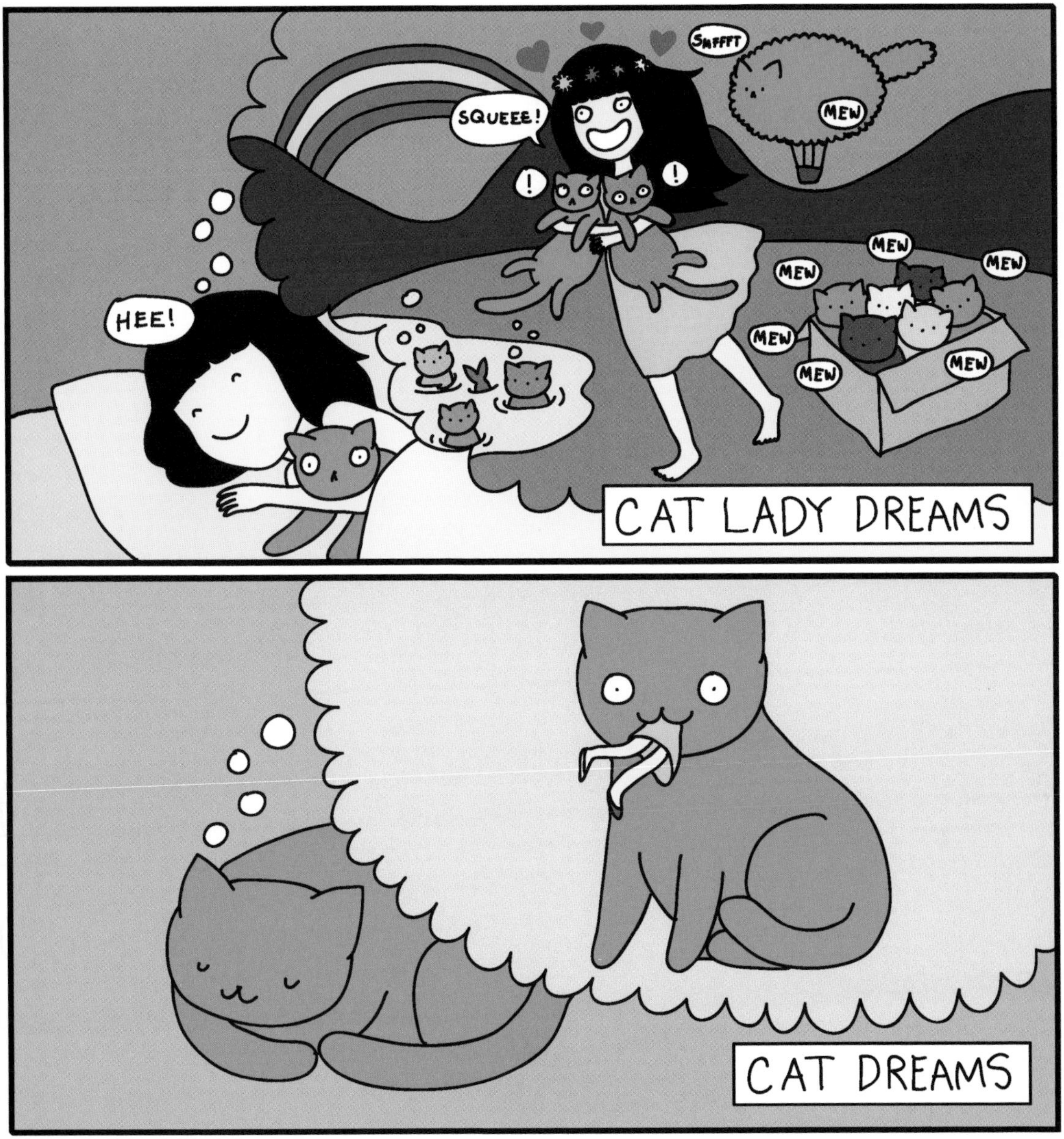
SQUEEE!
SNFFFT
MEW
!
!
HEE!
MEW
MEW
MEW
MEW
MEW
MEW
CAT LADY DREAMS
CAT DREAMS

You hired a chef for your kitty.
Fill out the menu of what will be served.

STARTERS:

MAIN COURSE:

SIDE DISHES:

DESSERTS:

DRINKS:

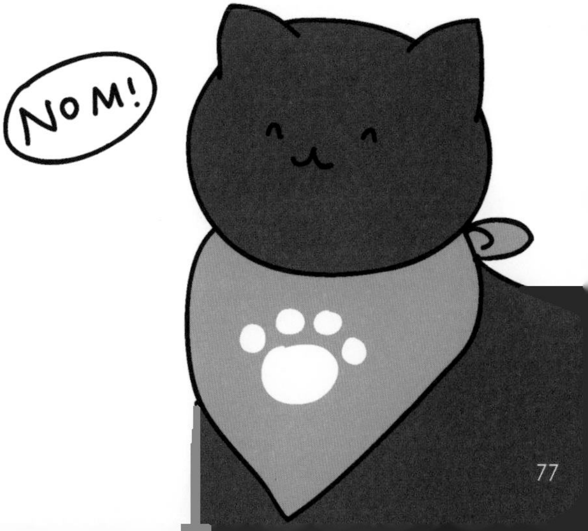
NOM!

Your current mood

○ HAPPY ○ EXCITED ○ HUNGRY ○ _ _ _ _ _ _ _ _ _ _

○ SAD ○ BORED ○ FULL

○ ECSTATIC ○ SLEEPY ○ SILLY

○ DEPRESSED ○ ENERGETIC ○ BUSY

○ INDIFFERENT ○ TIRED ○ GRUMPY

○ APATHETIC ○ ANGRY ○ OPTIMISTIC

ADD FACE (AND HAIR)

_ _ _ _ _ _ _ _'s current mood

○ CRAZY ○ AFFECTIONATE ○ HAPPY ○ _ _ _ _ _ _ _ _ _ _

○ CONTENT ○ ENERGETIC ○ ALERT

○ KINDA MEH ○ JUMPY ○ FRANTIC

○ SLEEPY ○ PLAYFUL ○ RELAXED

○ HUNGRY ○ FRIGHTENED ○ DEPRESSED

○ STALKER-Y ○ ANGRY ○ EXCITED

ADD FACE (AND MARKINGS)

DATE: _ _ _ _ _ _ _ _ _ _

YOU ARE THE JANE GOODALL OF THE DOMESTICATED CAT WORLD

What is the cat doing at this moment?

☐ sleeping

☐ demanding to be fed

☐ staring at the wall

☐ puking hairballs

☐ hunting

☐ cuddling with me

☐ avoiding me

☐ destroying something

☐ being playful

☐ I have absolutely no clue where (s)he is at this time

☐ looking down on me

☐ shedding on my clothes

☐ running around

☐ _ _ _ _ _ _ _ _ _ _ _ _ _ _ _ _ _ _ _

☐ _ _ _ _ _ _ _ _ _ _ _ _ _ _ _ _ _ _ _

ADD YOUR OBSERVATIONS

Write your favorite
quote about felines

WHAT DO YOU THINK
OF TOE FLOOFS?

🐾 What the heck are toe floofs?!

🐾 They are the cutest, most adorable thing ever!!!

🐾 Meh.

Make a list of some of your fondest memories

DRAW THE TASTIEST KITTY MEAL YOU COULD EVER THINK OF

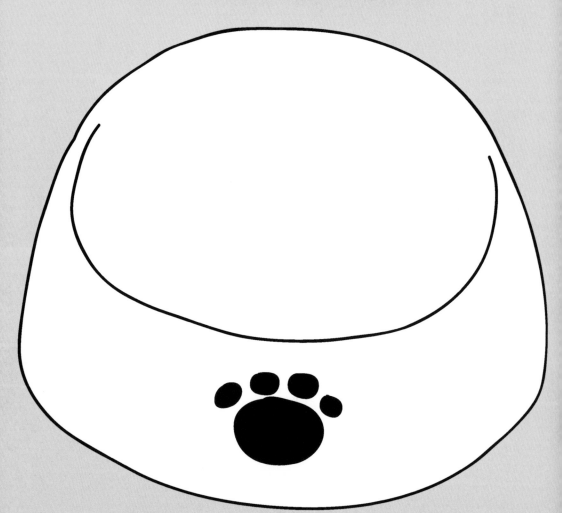

THINGS YOU (AND YOUR CAT) LIKE TO EAT

Wonderful FLUFF

PLACE A BAGGIE OF FUR HERE

RANDOM
THOUGHT
of the DAY

date:_____

YOU CHANCE UPON A GENIE WHO GRANTS YOU 3 WISHES, WHAT WOULD THEY BE?

IT TURNS OUT, THE GENIE ALSO LOVES CATS, AND HAS GRANTED 3 WISHES FOR YOUR FURRY FRIEND AS WELL. WHAT WOULD HIS/HER WISHES BE?

COMPOSE A HAIKU

High Five!

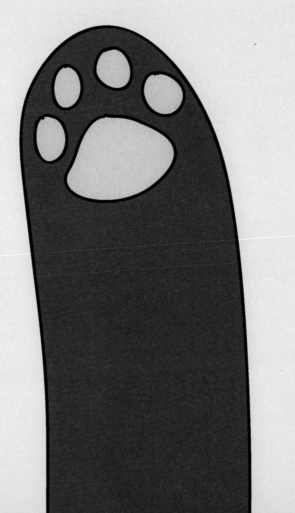

HUMAN PRINTS

Make markings of your hand here

PAW PRINTS!
add markings of ---------------'s paws here

Happiness is:

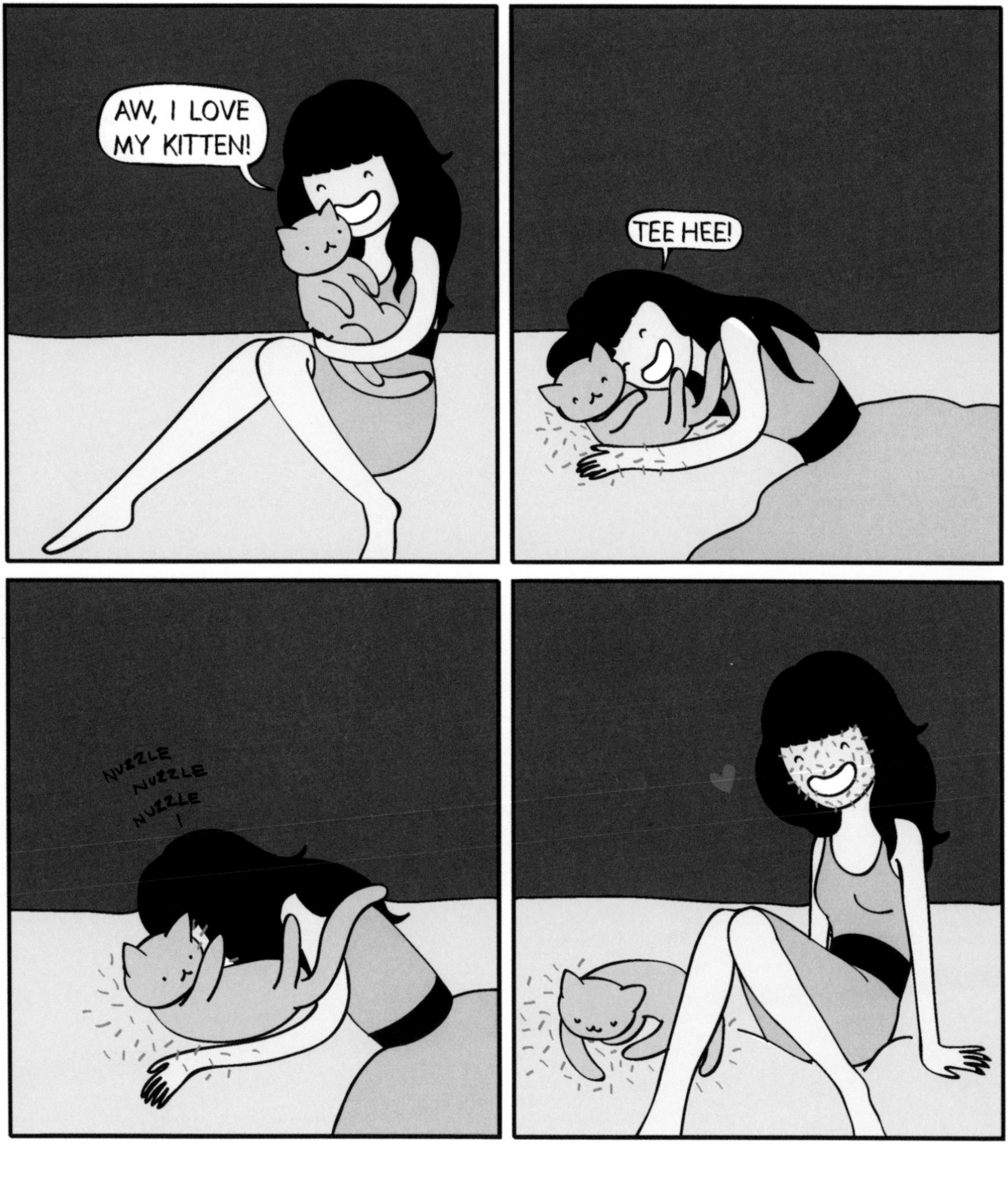
AW, I LOVE MY KITTEN!
TEE HEE!
NUZZLE NUZZLE NUZZLE

WHAT ARE _____'S NOT-SO-HIDDEN TALENTS?

WHAT ARE YOUR HIDDEN TALENTS?

Your current mood

- ◯ HAPPY
- ◯ SAD
- ◯ ECSTATIC
- ◯ DEPRESSED
- ◯ INDIFFERENT
- ◯ APATHETIC

- ◯ EXCITED
- ◯ BORED
- ◯ SLEEPY
- ◯ ENERGETIC
- ◯ TIRED
- ◯ ANGRY

- ◯ HUNGRY
- ◯ FULL
- ◯ SILLY
- ◯ BUSY
- ◯ GRUMPY
- ◯ OPTIMISTIC

◯ _ _ _ _ _ _ _ _ _ _ _ _ _

ADD FACE (AND HAIR)

_ _ _ _ _ _ _ _'s current mood

- ◯ CRAZY
- ◯ CONTENT
- ◯ KINDA MEH
- ◯ SLEEPY
- ◯ HUNGRY
- ◯ STALKER-Y

- ◯ AFFECTIONATE
- ◯ ENERGETIC
- ◯ JUMPY
- ◯ PLAYFUL
- ◯ FRIGHTENED
- ◯ ANGRY

- ◯ HAPPY
- ◯ ALERT
- ◯ FRANTIC
- ◯ RELAXED
- ◯ DEPRESSED
- ◯ EXCITED

◯ _ _ _ _ _ _ _ _ _ _ _ _ _

ADD FACE (AND MARKINGS)

DATE: _ _ _ _ _ _ _ _ _ _ _

YOU ARE THE JANE GOODALL OF THE DOMESTICATED CAT WORLD

What is the cat doing at this moment?

- ☐ sleeping
- ☐ demanding to be fed
- ☐ staring at the wall
- ☐ puking hairballs
- ☐ hunting
- ☐ cuddling with me
- ☐ avoiding me
- ☐ destroying something
- ☐ being playful
- ☐ I have absolutely no clue where (s)he is at this time
- ☐ looking down on me
- ☐ shedding on my clothes
- ☐ running around
- ☐ _
- ☐ _

ADD YOUR OBSERVATIONS

99

How my cats see me

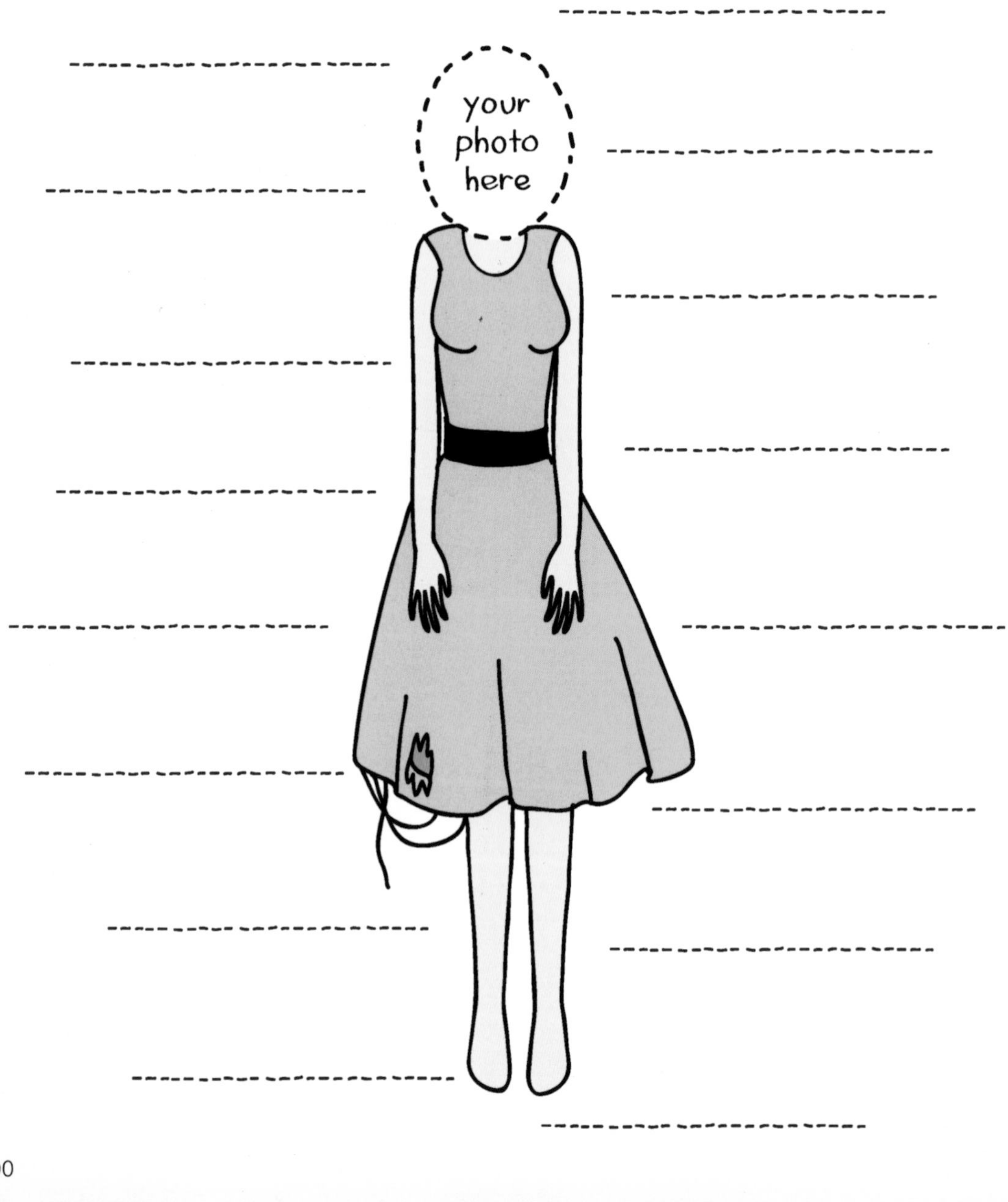
your
photo
here

How I see my cats

HOW MANY PHOTOS OF YOUR CAT(S) DO YOU HAVE IN YOUR PHONE?

AND HOW LIKELY IS THAT NUMBER > 100?

SHARE YOUR MOST FAVORITES HERE

IT'S CAT O'CLOCK.
GIVE YOUR CAT A HUG!

THE CARDBOARD BOX, IT TURNS OUT,
IS A PORTAL TO ANOTHER REALM.
WHERE DOES IT LEAD TO?

IF YOUR CAT WAS A PERSON, WHAT KIND OF PERSON WOULD (S)HE BE?

date: _____

RANDOM THOUGHT
of the DAY

107

HUMAN BADGES

Cross out the badge(s) you win today

DIDN'T
OVERSLEEP

CAT VIDEO
ENTHUSIAST

LITTER BOX
CUSTODIAN

HUMAN
PILLOW

TOY FETCHER
AND PICKER UPPERER

BELLY
SCRATCHER

SPILL WIPER

CARDBOARD BOX
PROVIDER

MASTER
CUDDLER

CAT PHOTO
"LIKER"

CUSHION
FLUFFER

FOSTER FAILURE
WINNER

FOOD DISPENSER

BOOP
EXPERT

FLUFF
TAMER

FURRY WARDROBE
WEARER

CATNIP DEALER

CAREGIVER OF
THE YEAR

What is your least favorite part about your body?

It's okay, cats love you
just the same.

HOW MANY CATS DO YOU HAVE, AND WHY DO YOU WANT MORE?

The cat just stepped on your keyboard. What appeared on the screen?

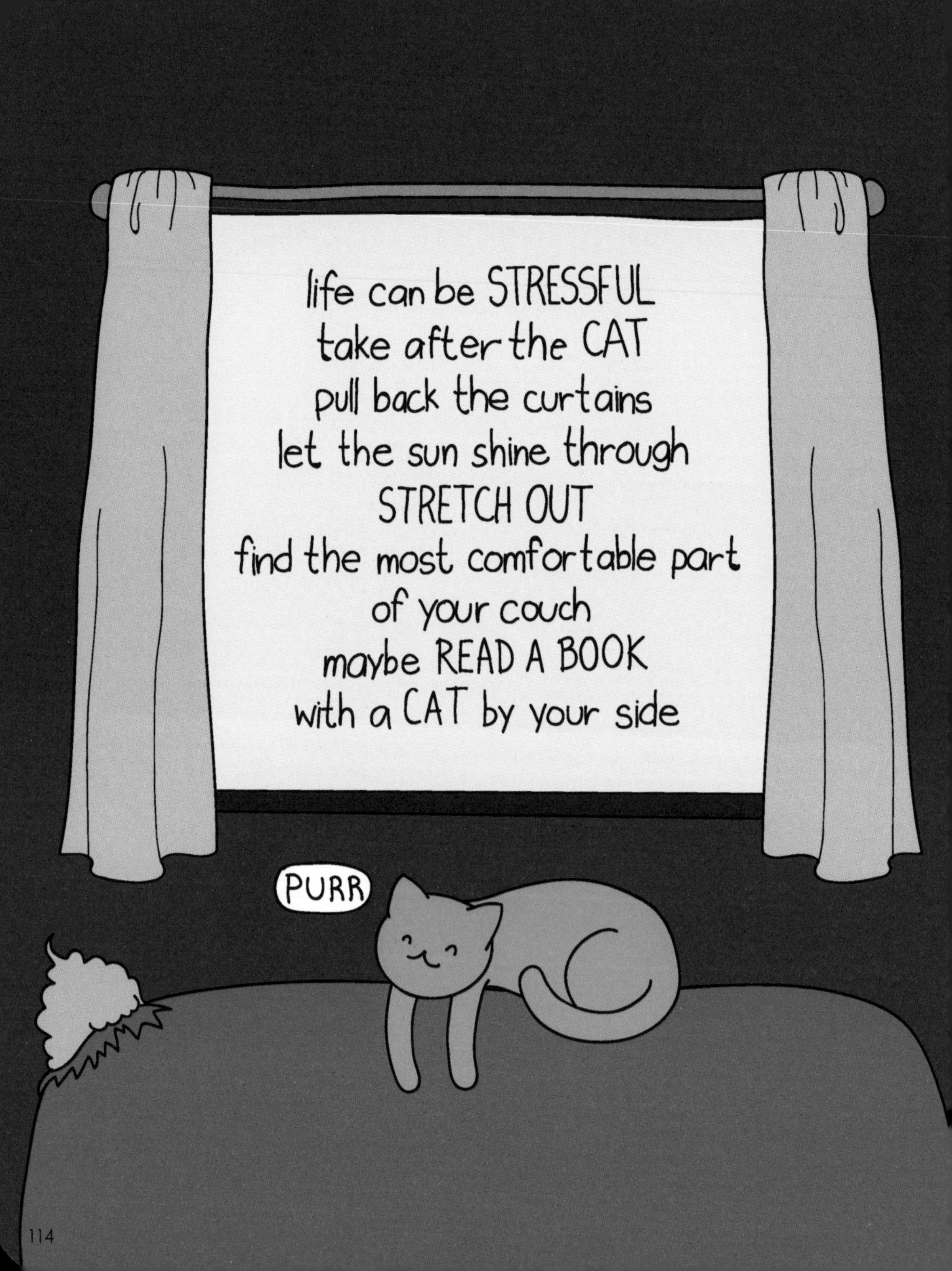
life can be STRESSFUL
take after the CAT
pull back the curtains
let the sun shine through
STRETCH OUT
find the most comfortable part
of your couch
maybe READ A BOOK
with a CAT by your side
PURR

Describe ______________'s meows

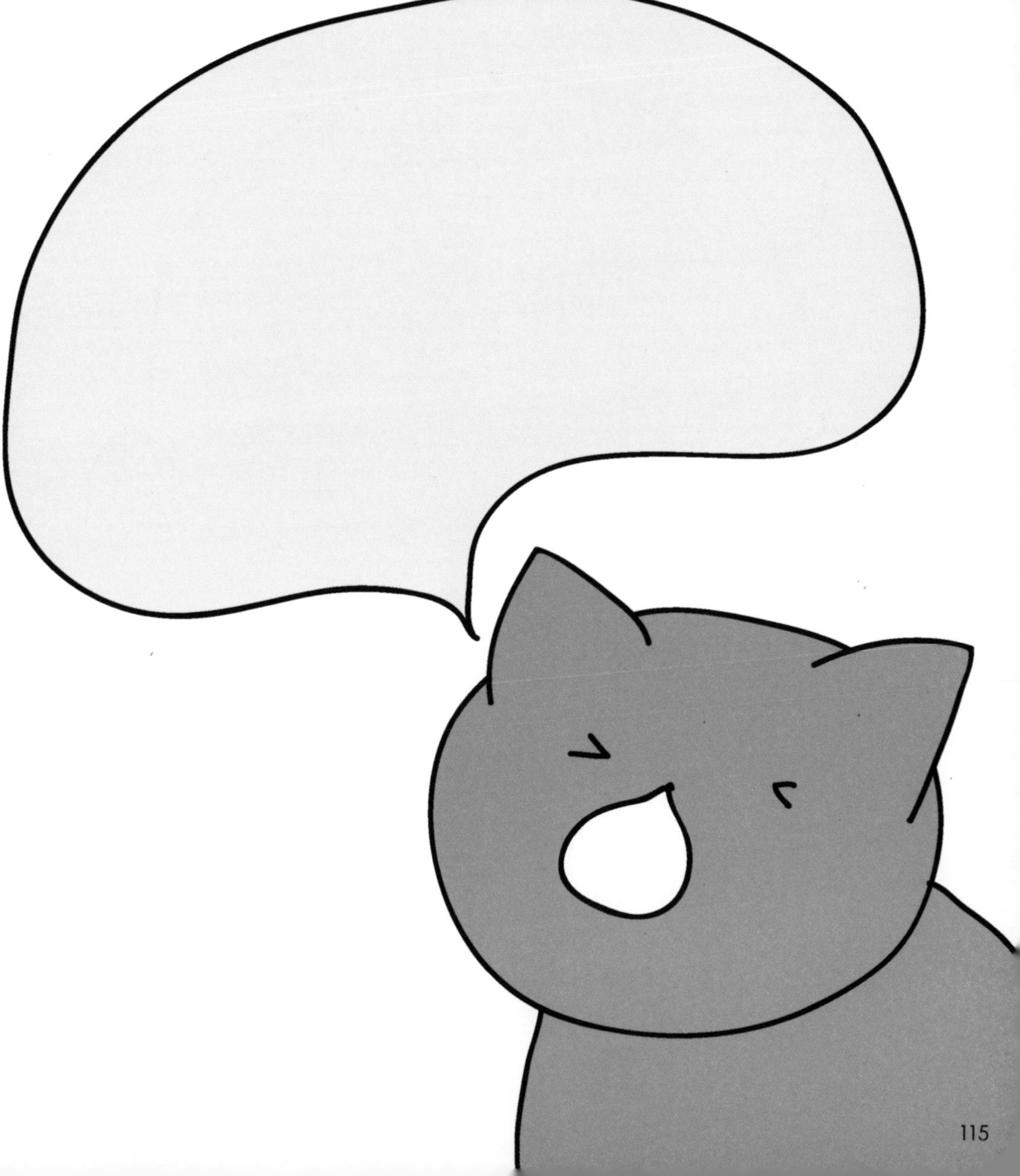

IF YOUR CAT WERE TO GIVE YOU A NAME,
WHAT WOULD IT BE?

HOW DID YOU COME ABOUT PICKING
YOUR CAT'S NAME?

DOES IT MEAN SOMETHING?

Your current mood

- ○ HAPPY
- ○ SAD
- ○ ECSTATIC
- ○ DEPRESSED
- ○ INDIFFERENT
- ○ APATHETIC

- ○ EXCITED
- ○ BORED
- ○ SLEEPY
- ○ ENERGETIC
- ○ TIRED
- ○ ANGRY

- ○ HUNGRY
- ○ FULL
- ○ SILLY
- ○ BUSY
- ○ GRUMPY
- ○ OPTIMISTIC

- ○ _____

ADD FACE (AND HAIR)

_____'s current mood

- ○ CRAZY
- ○ CONTENT
- ○ KINDA MEH
- ○ SLEEPY
- ○ HUNGRY
- ○ STALKER-Y

- ○ AFFECTIONATE
- ○ ENERGETIC
- ○ JUMPY
- ○ PLAYFUL
- ○ FRIGHTENED
- ○ ANGRY

- ○ HAPPY
- ○ ALERT
- ○ FRANTIC
- ○ RELAXED
- ○ DEPRESSED
- ○ EXCITED

- ○ _____

ADD FACE (AND MARKINGS)

DATE: _____

YOU ARE THE JANE GOODALL OF THE DOMESTICATED CAT WORLD

What is the cat doing at this moment?

ADD YOUR OBSERVATIONS

- ☐ sleeping
- ☐ demanding to be fed
- ☐ staring at the wall
- ☐ puking hairballs
- ☐ hunting
- ☐ cuddling with me
- ☐ avoiding me
- ☐ destroying something
- ☐ being playful
- ☐ I have absolutely no clue where (s)he is at this time
- ☐ looking down on me
- ☐ shedding on my clothes
- ☐ running around
- ☐ _____
- ☐ _____

119

TAKE A MAGIC CARDBOARD BOX RIDE
TO PLACES YOU'D LOVE TO VISIT!

On a scale of 1-10

ARE YOU A STEREOTYPICAL CRAZY CAT LADY?

◯ ◯ ◯ ◯ ◯ ◯ ◯ ◯ ◯ ◯
1   2   3   4   5   6   7   8   9   10

HOW MUCH DO YOU LOVE YOUR CAT?

◯ ◯ ◯ ◯ ◯ ◯ ◯ ◯ ◯ ◯
1   2   3   4   5   6   7   8   9   10

HOW OFTEN DO YOU THINK OF YOUR CAT(S)?

◯ ◯ ◯ ◯ ◯ ◯ ◯ ◯ ◯ ◯
1   2   3   4   5   6   7   8   9   10

DO YOU SEE YOUR CAT(S) ON THE SAME
LEVEL AS YOUR HUMAN FRIENDS?

◯ ◯ ◯ ◯ ◯ ◯ ◯ ◯ ◯ ◯
1   2   3   4   5   6   7   8   9   10

DO YOU SEE YOURSELF TAKING IN ANOTHER
CAT INTO YOUR LIFE IN THE FUTURE?

◯ ◯ ◯ ◯ ◯ ◯ ◯ ◯ ◯ ◯
1 2 3 4 5 6 7 8 9 10

HOW EXCITED DO YOU GET WHEN YOU SEE
YOUR CAT(S) WHEN YOU GET HOME FROM WORK?

◯ ◯ ◯ ◯ ◯ ◯ ◯ ◯ ◯ ◯
1 2 3 4 5 6 7 8 9 10

DO YOU TALK ABOUT CAT(S) OFTEN?

◯ ◯ ◯ ◯ ◯ ◯ ◯ ◯ ◯ ◯
1 2 3 4 5 6 7 8 9 10

DO YOU PREFER CAT(S) TO HUMANS?

◯ ◯ ◯ ◯ ◯ ◯ ◯ ◯ ◯ ◯
1 2 3 4 5 6 7 8 9 10

DESCRIBE YOURSELF IN ONE WORD

DESCRIBE _____ IN ONE WORD

124

What is your least favorite bit about _____?

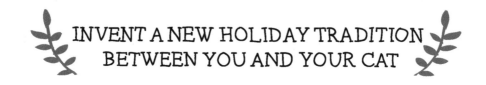
What is the holiday about?

What kinds of decorations will be put up?

What kinds of food will you prepare?

Will you invite guests?

who will you invite? And will there be presents?

THINGS .... HAS KNOCKED OVER TODAY

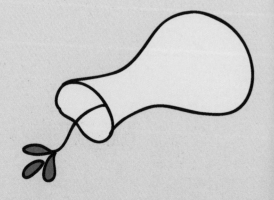

RANDOM
THOUGHT
OF THE DAY

DRAW YOUR
Stick FIGURE
FAMILY

FURRY (AND NOT-SO-FURRY) FRIENDS INCLUDED

Random Thought of the Day

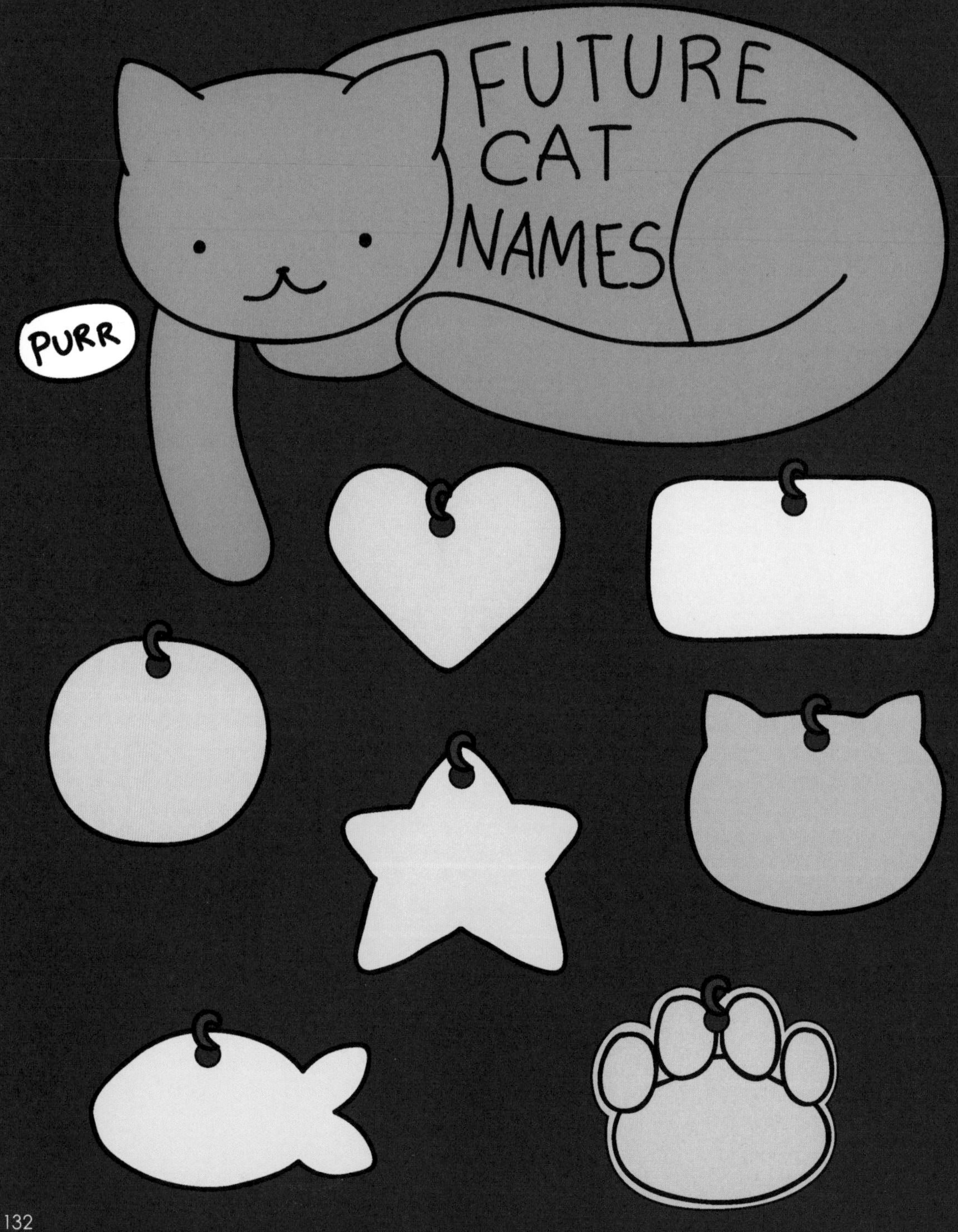
FUTURE CAT NAMES
PURR

DESCRIBE YOUR PURRFECT DAY

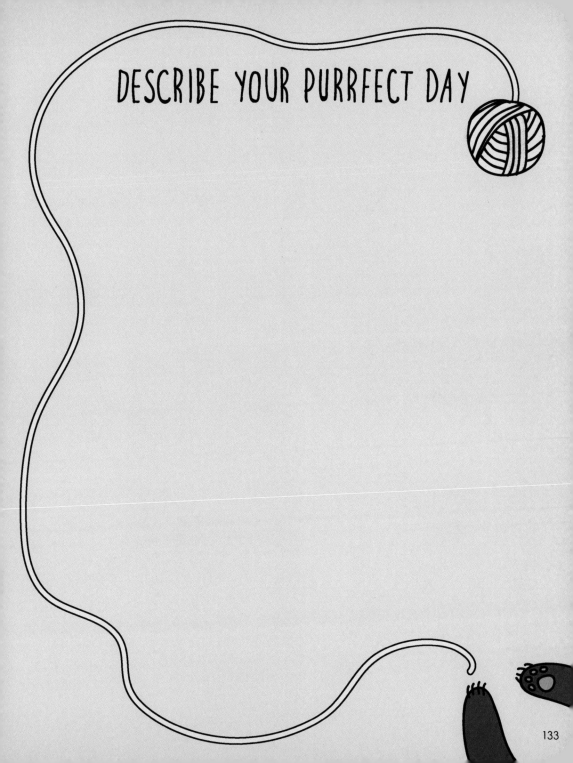

Cross out any of the items you've gotten as presents

HI!

134

DRAW OR CREATE A LIST OF PRESENTS
YOU'VE GOTTEN FROM THE CAT

Share the most photogenic photo of yourself

PLACE PHOTO HERE

Share the most photogenic photo of your cat

PLACE PHOTO HERE

Listen to your cat purr

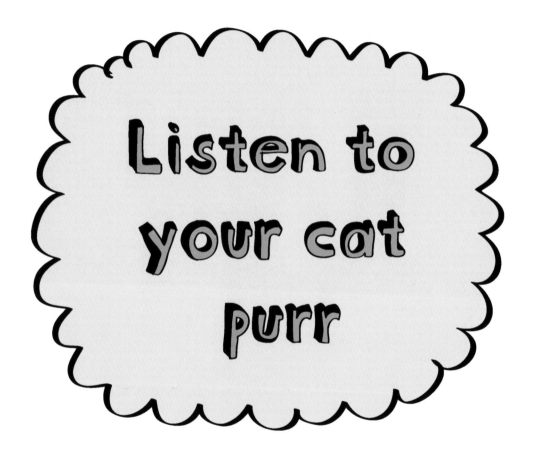

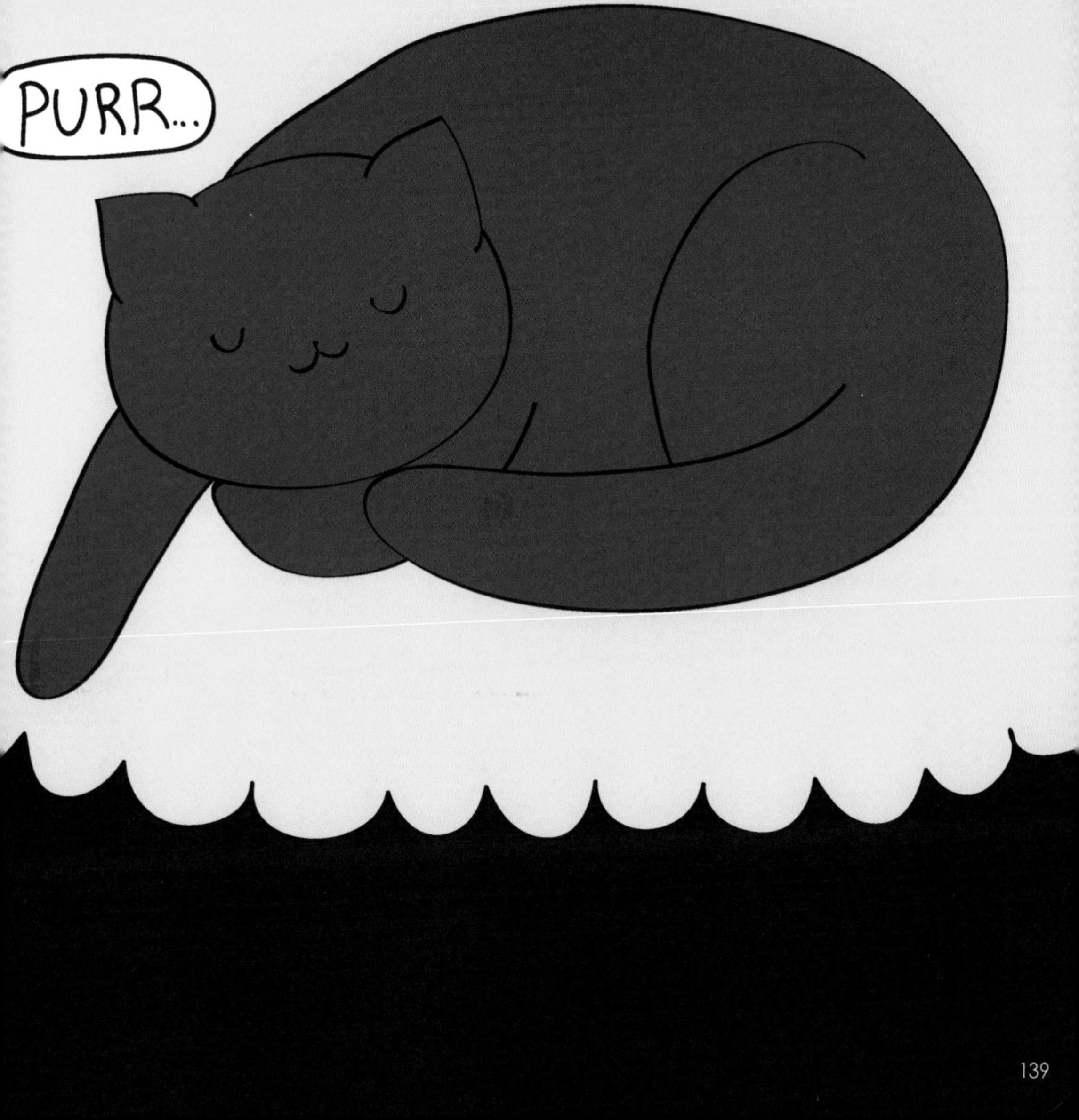
PURR...

SPEND SOME QUALITY TIME WITH YOUR FURRY FRIEND.

THINGS THAT SCARE YOU

THINGS THAT SCARE _____

Attach your most recent receipt of items you've purchased for yourself

Attach your most recent pet supply/food receipt

WHAT'S TYPICALLY IN YOUR PANTRY?

CAT PERSON'S PANTRY

CANS OF TUNA. MAYBE FOR HUMAN. MAYBE FOR CAT. OR BOTH.

ALL SORTS OF WET FOOD...

...BECAUSE THE CATS ACT LIKE THEY LOVE ME MORE WHEN I GIVE THEM WET FOOD

CAT FOOD I FORGOT I HAD SO THEY ACCUMULATED IN THE PANTRY'S NETHER REGIONS

COLLECTION OF CAT TREATS THE CATS HATE

CAT TREATS THE CATS LOVE UNTIL THEY DECIDE THAT THEY HATE IT

PLASTIC BINS SO THE CATS CAN'T GET TO THEM

DRY CAT FOOD THE CATS LOVE AND STUFF THEMSELVES WITH UNTIL THEY THROW UP ON THE CARPET

EXTREMELY EXPENSIVE AND SUPPOSEDLY HEALTHY CAT FOOD NO ONE WANTS TO EAT (BUT I SNEAK IN THEIR BOWLS WHICH THEY EAT AROUND ANYWAY)

COLLECTION OF CAT FOOD THE CATS HATE, NOT EVEN THE STRAYS WOULD TOUCH IT

CAT FOOD FOR STRAYS

COMPLETE THIS SELF-PORTRAIT

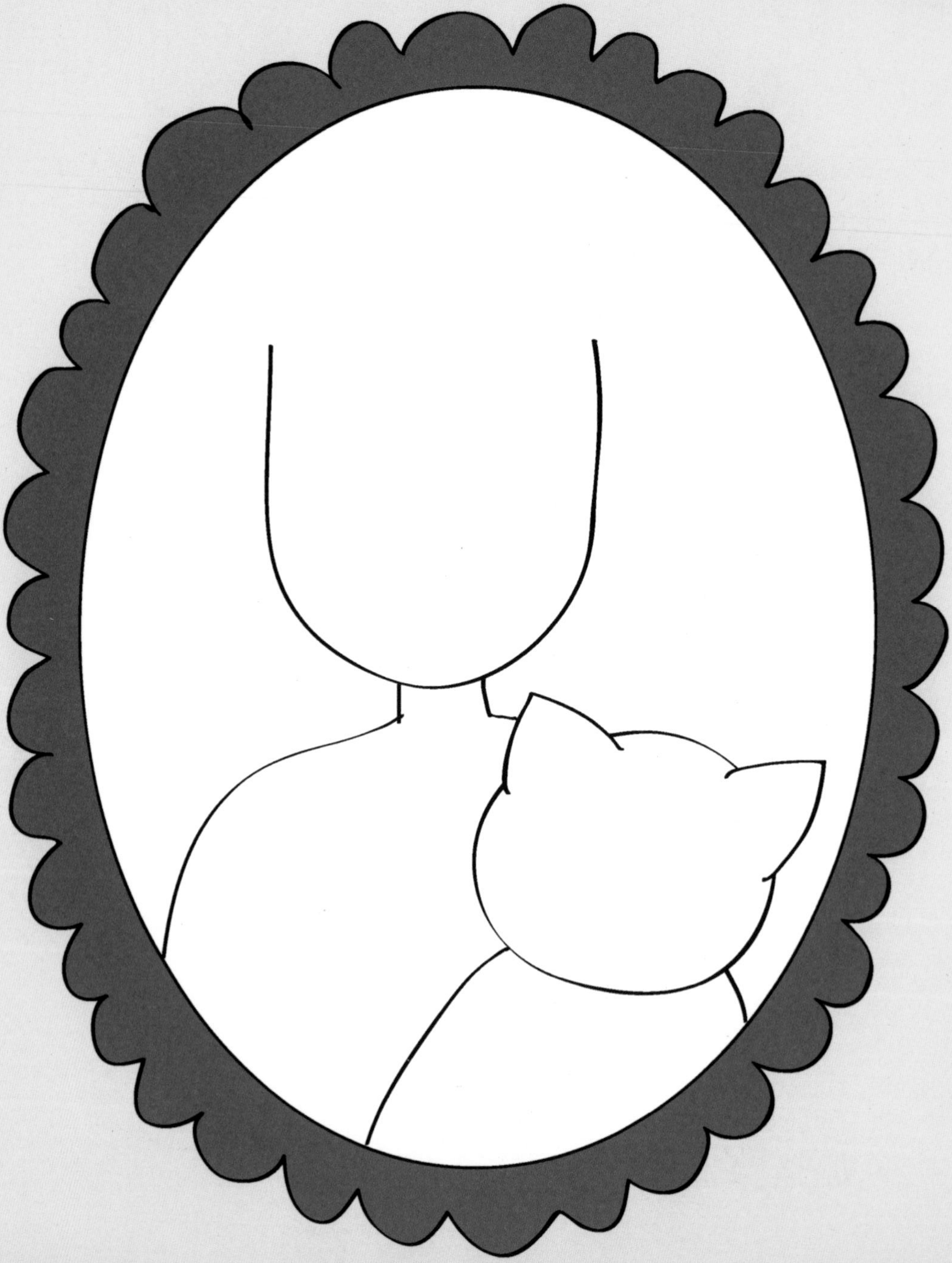

Fill this bell jar with things that remind you of your KITTY

147

DO YOU HAVE A SIGNIFICANT OTHER?

If yes, is (s)he a cat person?

If yes, how many cats does (s)he have?

If no, does (s)he like having pets?

If no, how do you get along?

What other interests do you have together?

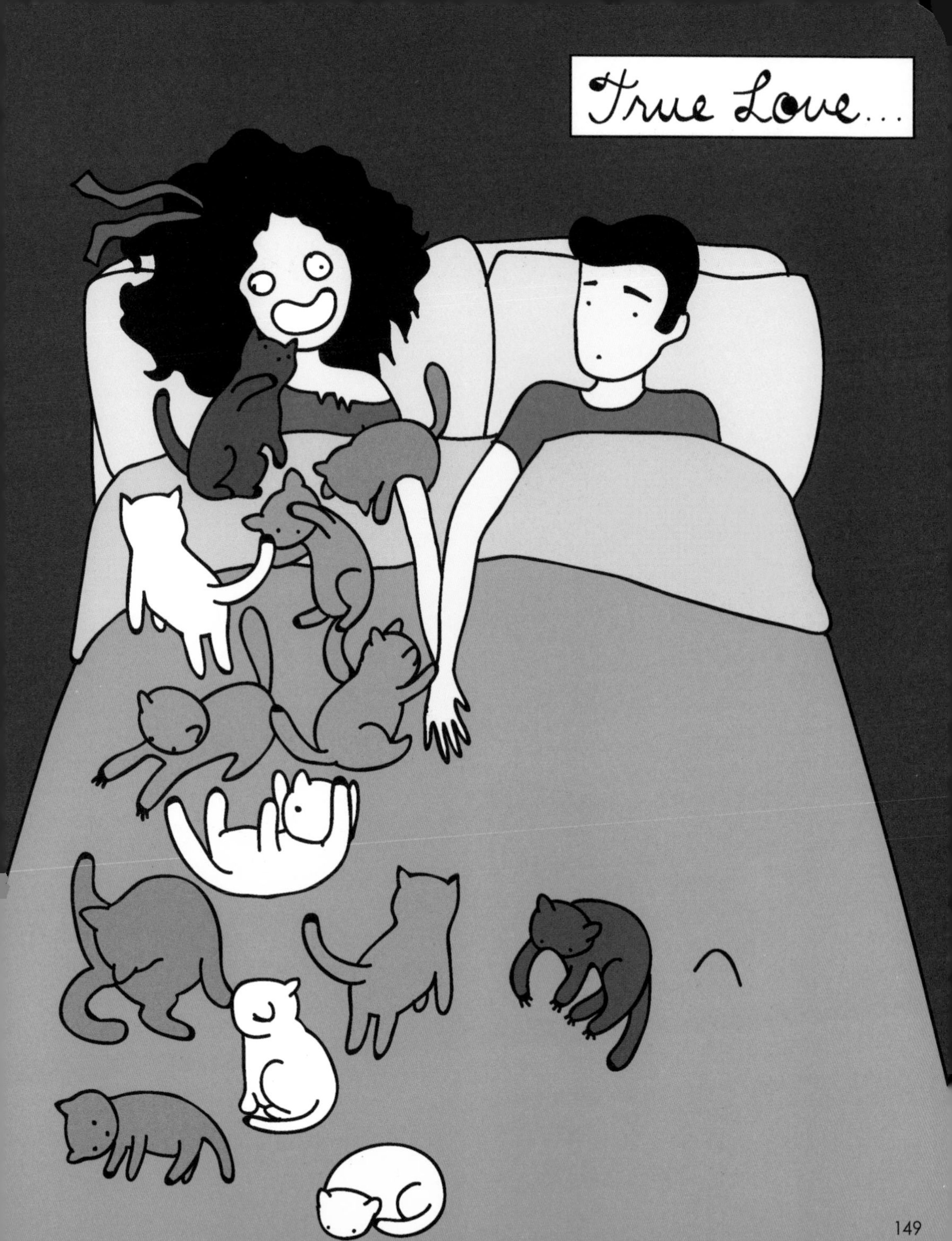
True Love...

Your cat is a superhero, and you are his/her sidekick. What kinds of heroic deeds do you go about doing?

date:------------

RANDOM THOUGHT of the DAY

151

SHOPPING CHECK LIST

- [ ] CAT FOOD
  (THAT THE CAT ACTUALLY LIKES THIS TIME)
- [ ] WINE
- [ ] CAT LITTER
- [ ] ~~A NEW CAT BED~~
  FIND A CARDBOARD BOX
- [ ] CANS OF TUNA (FOR ME AND THE CAT)
- [ ] ~~TOYS~~
  FIND ANOTHER CARDBOARD BOX
- [ ] WINE
- [ ] ----------------------------------
- [ ] ----------------------------------
- [ ] ----------------------------------
- [ ] ----------------------------------
- [ ] ----------------------------------
- [ ] ----------------------------------

- [ ] ------------------------------------
- [ ] ------------------------------------
- [ ] ------------------------------------
- [ ] ------------------------------------
- [ ] ------------------------------------
- [ ] ------------------------------------
- [ ] ------------------------------------
- [ ] ------------------------------------
- [ ] ------------------------------------
- [ ] ------------------------------------
- [ ] ------------------------------------
- [ ] ------------------------------------
- [ ] ------------------------------------
- [ ] ------------------------------------
- [ ] ------------------------------------

IT'S A RAINY DAY, AND YOU'RE STUCK AT HOME.

WHAT ARE YOU WATCHING?

ARE YOU ON THE COMPUTER?

WHAT ARE YOU BROWSING?

ARE YOU TAKING A NAP?

WHAT ARE YOU READING?

WHAT ARE YOU DRINKING?

WHAT ARE YOU SNACKING ON?

DO YOU NEED TO GO TO THE BATHROOM?

SORRY, ALL THE KITTIES ARE ON YOU.
MAYBE A LITTLE BIT LATER.

What is the first thing that pops in your head when you see these objects?

You can read the minds of cats. What is _____ thinking of right now?

THINGS CATS DESTROY BUT SHOULDN'T

Cross out the items your cat has destroyed

DRAW OR CREATE A LIST OF THINGS THE
CAT LIKES TO DESTROY

STOP for a minute, and give your cat a TREAT

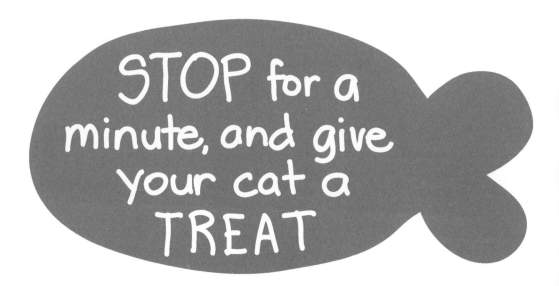

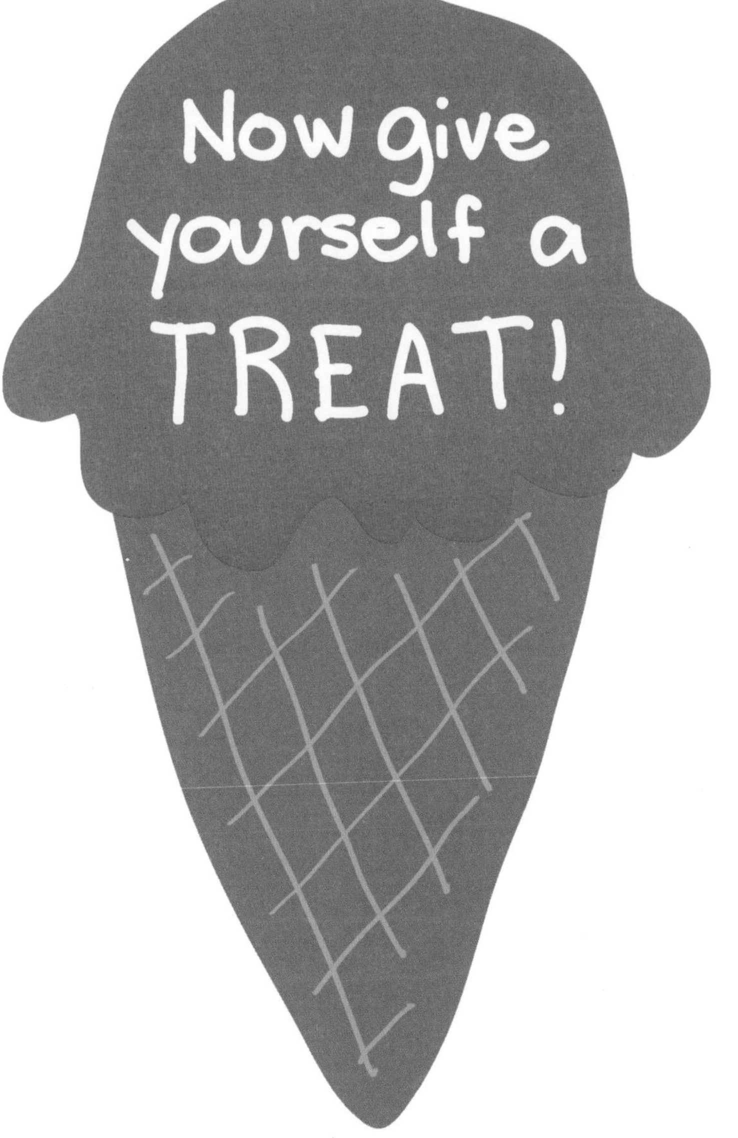
Now give
yourself a
TREAT!

Your current mood

- ○ HAPPY
- ○ SAD
- ○ ECSTATIC
- ○ DEPRESSED
- ○ INDIFFERENT
- ○ APATHETIC

- ○ EXCITED
- ○ BORED
- ○ SLEEPY
- ○ ENERGETIC
- ○ TIRED
- ○ ANGRY

- ○ HUNGRY
- ○ FULL
- ○ SILLY
- ○ BUSY
- ○ GRUMPY
- ○ OPTIMISTIC

- ○ _ _ _ _ _ _ _ _ _ _ _ _ _

ADD FACE (AND HAIR)

_ _ _ _ _ _ _'s current mood

- ○ CRAZY
- ○ CONTENT
- ○ KINDA MEH
- ○ SLEEPY
- ○ HUNGRY
- ○ STALKER-Y

- ○ AFFECTIONATE
- ○ ENERGETIC
- ○ JUMPY
- ○ PLAYFUL
- ○ FRIGHTENED
- ○ ANGRY

- ○ HAPPY
- ○ ALERT
- ○ FRANTIC
- ○ RELAXED
- ○ DEPRESSED
- ○ EXCITED

- ○ _ _ _ _ _ _ _ _ _ _ _ _ _

ADD FACE (AND MARKINGS)

DATE: _ _ _ _ _ _ _ _ _ _

YOU ARE THE JANE GOODALL OF THE DOMESTICATED CAT WORLD

What is the cat doing at this moment?

- ☐ sleeping
- ☐ demanding to be fed
- ☐ staring at the wall
- ☐ puking hairballs
- ☐ hunting
- ☐ cuddling with me
- ☐ avoiding me
- ☐ destroying something
- ☐ being playful
- ☐ I have absolutely no clue where (s)he is at this time
- ☐ looking down on me
- ☐ shedding on my clothes
- ☐ running around
- ☐ _____
- ☐ _____

ADD YOUR OBSERVATIONS

UNFORGETTABLE MOMENTS

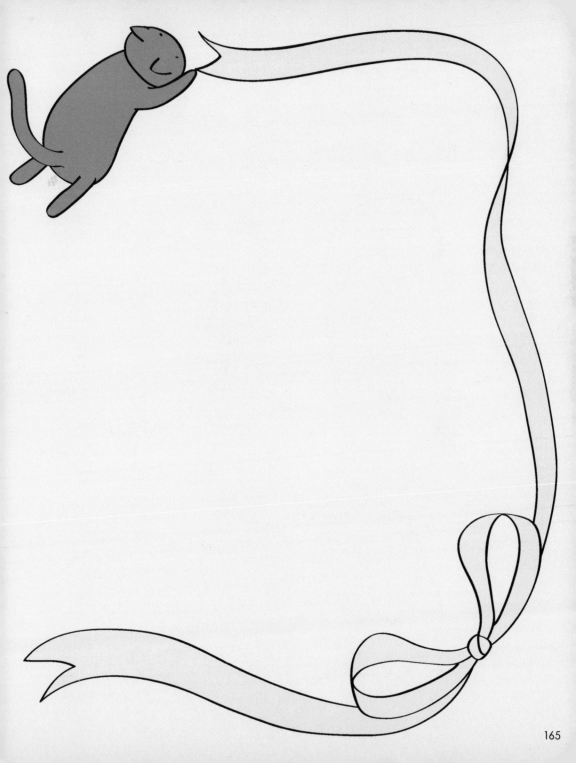

Your cat has given you some Valentine's Day candy. What does it say on each one?

You've given your cat some Valentine's Day Candy. What does it say on each one?

A TRIP TO THE VET

How is _____ doing?

What is the trip for?

How is (s)he around the vet?

What is his/her weight?

What medicines does she/he take?

How is (s)he feeling?

Notes:

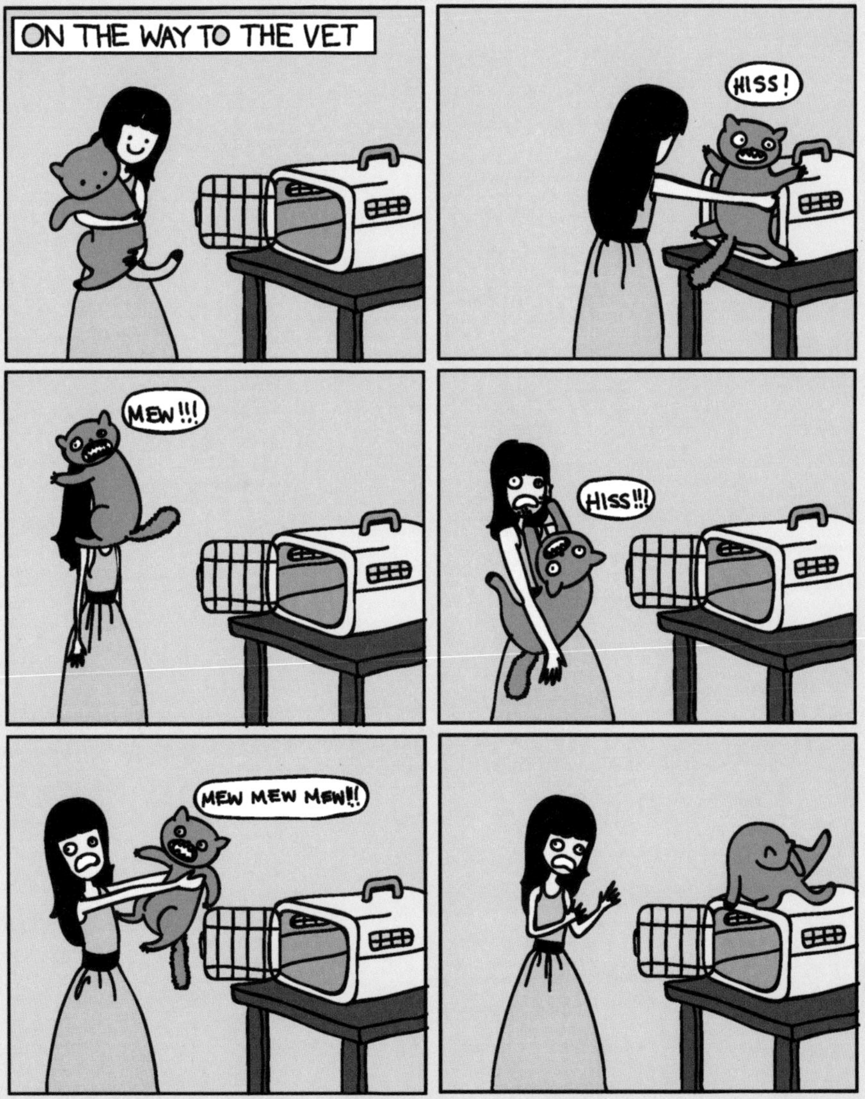
ON THE WAY TO THE VET
HISS!
MEW!!!
HISS!!!
MEW MEW MEW!!

Write a letter to your best friend

date:_____

RANDOM THOUGHT of the DAY

Have you tried "walking" your cat outdoors? What was that like?

My Whisker Collection

PLACE A BAGGIE OF
SHED WHISKERS HERE

WHAT ARE SOME WEIRD AND CRAZY THINGS YOUR CAT DOES?

HOW TO TELL WHEN YOUR CAT IS CRAZY

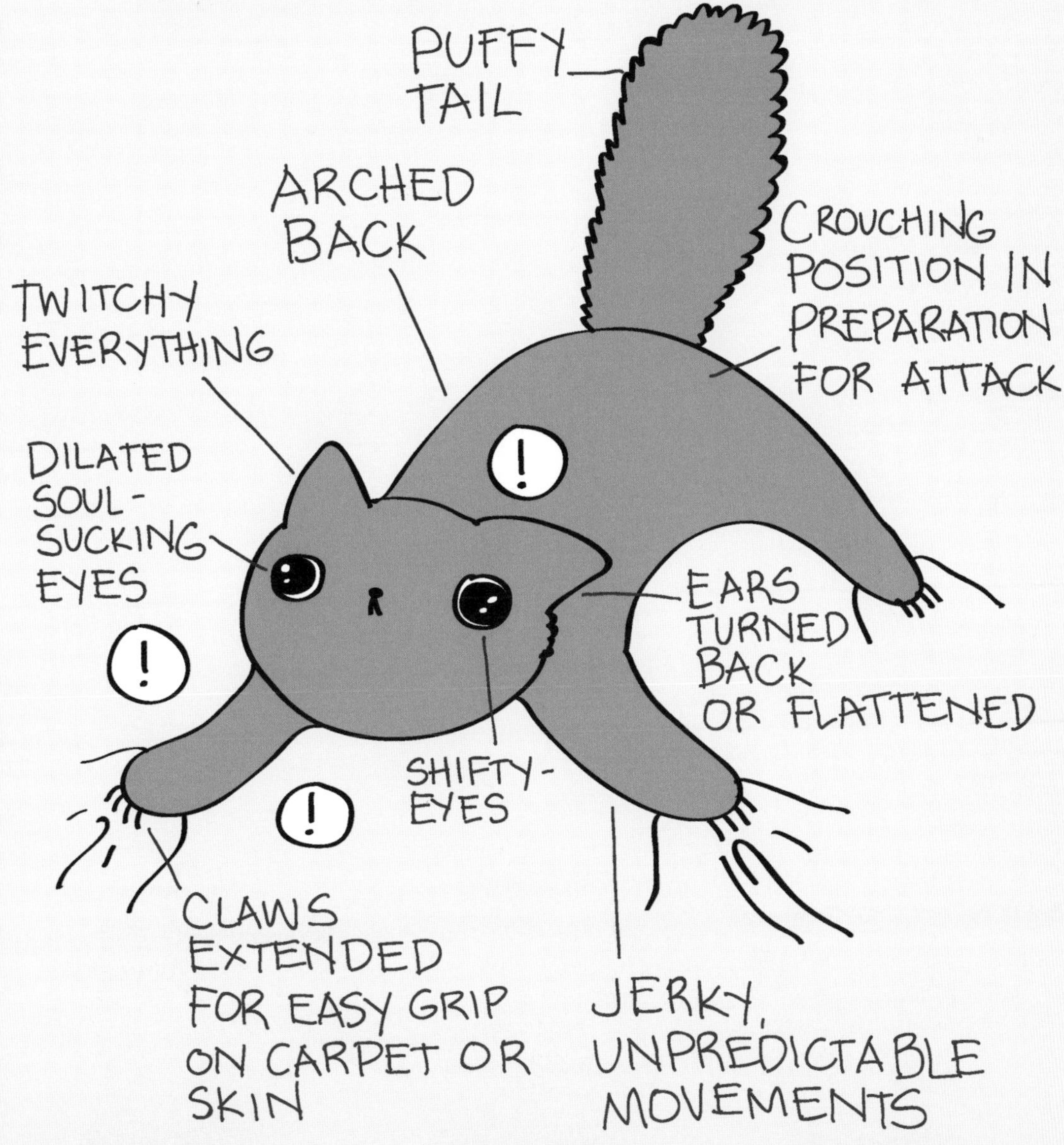
PUFFY TAIL
ARCHED BACK
CROUCHING POSITION IN PREPARATION FOR ATTACK
TWITCHY EVERYTHING
DILATED SOUL-SUCKING EYES
!
!
!
EARS TURNED BACK OR FLATTENED
SHIFTY-EYES
CLAWS EXTENDED FOR EASY GRIP ON CARPET OR SKIN
JERKY, UNPREDICTABLE MOVEMENTS

Who was your first cat?
Describe him/her, post a photo, or make
a collage of your moments together

WHO WINS THE **CAT** vs **HUMAN** OLYMPICS?

STARING COMPETITION

CAT OR HUMAN

THE LAZING AROUND COMPETITION

CAT OR HUMAN

THE NOT GIVING A CRAP COMPETITION

CAT OR HUMAN

THE ABILITY TO SLEEP ON RANDOM STUFF COMPETITION

CAT OR HUMAN

EATING COMPETITION

CAT OR HUMAN

HUNTING COMPETITION

CAT OR HUMAN

WHO LETS GO FIRST IN A SNUGGLE COMPETITION

CAT OR HUMAN

What would it say under your cat's yearbook picture?

Place
photo
here

NOW THAT WE KNOW YOUR CAT IS AWESOME. WHAT MAKES YOU SO AWESOME?

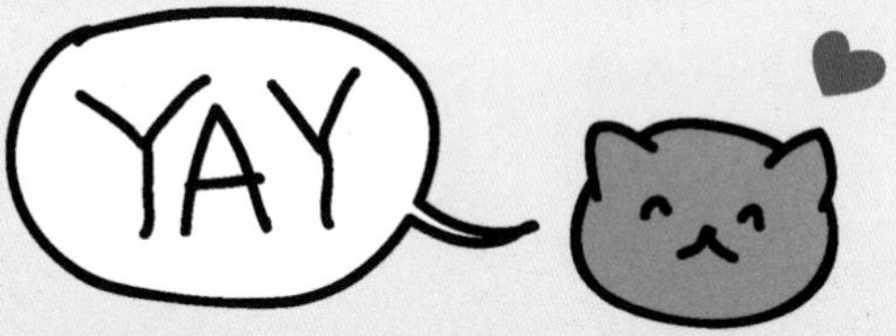
YAY

YOUR CAT IS A HIDE-AND-SEEK CHAMPION

List some favorite hiding spots

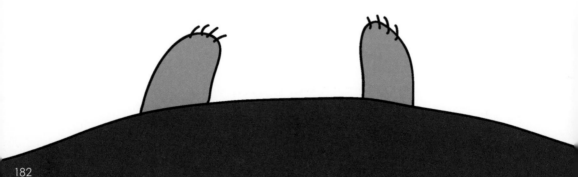

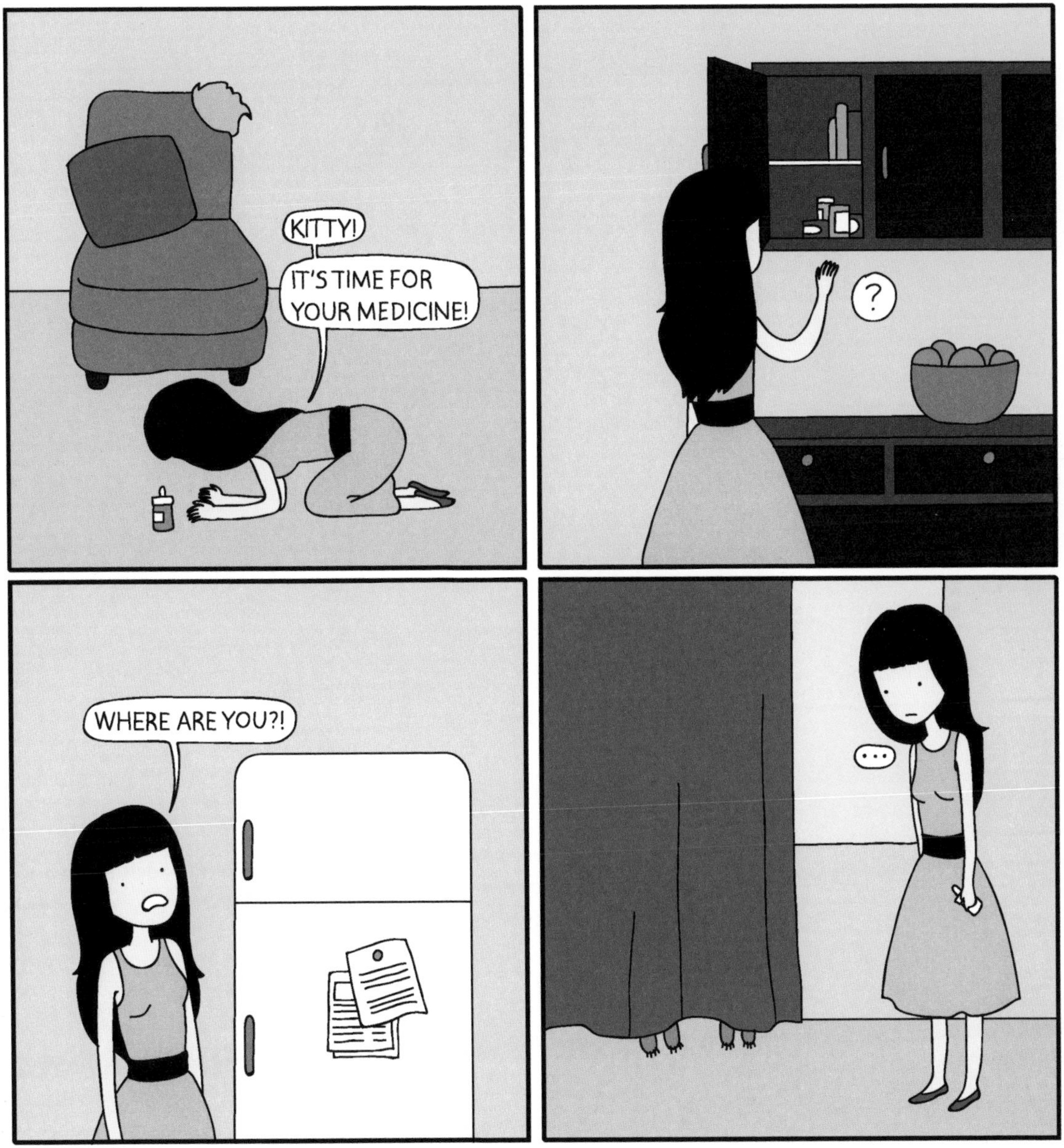
KITTY!
IT'S TIME FOR YOUR MEDICINE!
?
WHERE ARE YOU?!
...

WHAT'S YOUR FAVORITE MOVIE WITH CATS?

Kitty hates wearing clothes. But that won't stop you from designing the fanciest outfit!

IF YOU HAD THE ABILITY TO SPEAK WITH _____
WHAT WOULD YOUR CONVERSATIONS BE LIKE?

THE CAT LIKES TO TAKE NAPS
ON YOUR FAVORITE TOP.
DRAW A BUNCH OF FUR ON IT.

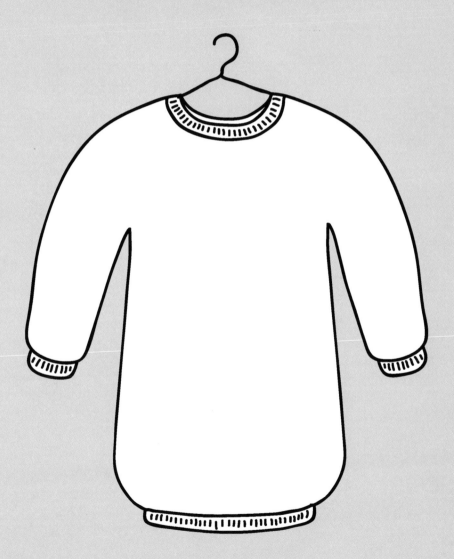

Your current mood

- ○ HAPPY
- ○ SAD
- ○ ECSTATIC
- ○ DEPRESSED
- ○ INDIFFERENT
- ○ APATHETIC

- ○ EXCITED
- ○ BORED
- ○ SLEEPY
- ○ ENERGETIC
- ○ TIRED
- ○ ANGRY

- ○ HUNGRY
- ○ FULL
- ○ SILLY
- ○ BUSY
- ○ GRUMPY
- ○ OPTIMISTIC

- ○ _____

ADD FACE (AND HAIR)

_____'s current mood

- ○ CRAZY
- ○ CONTENT
- ○ KINDA MEH
- ○ SLEEPY
- ○ HUNGRY
- ○ STALKER-Y

- ○ AFFECTIONATE
- ○ ENERGETIC
- ○ JUMPY
- ○ PLAYFUL
- ○ FRIGHTENED
- ○ ANGRY

- ○ HAPPY
- ○ ALERT
- ○ FRANTIC
- ○ RELAXED
- ○ DEPRESSED
- ○ EXCITED

- ○ _____

ADD FACE (AND MARKINGS)

DATE: _____

YOU ARE THE JANE GOODALL OF THE DOMESTICATED CAT WORLD

What is the cat doing at this moment?

- ☐ sleeping
- ☐ demanding to be fed
- ☐ staring at the wall
- ☐ puking hairballs
- ☐ hunting
- ☐ cuddling with me
- ☐ avoiding me
- ☐ destroying something
- ☐ being playful
- ☐ I have absolutely no clue where (s)he is at this time
- ☐ looking down on me
- ☐ shedding on my clothes
- ☐ running around
- ☐ _____
- ☐ _____

ADD YOUR OBSERVATIONS

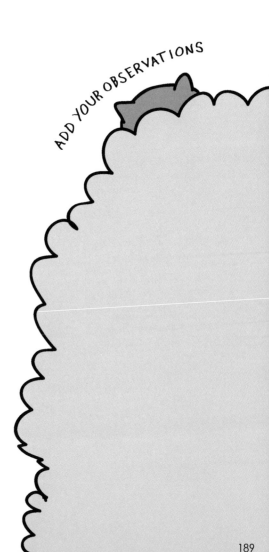

HELLO,
my name is:

And I'm a Cat Person

A Brief Autobiography

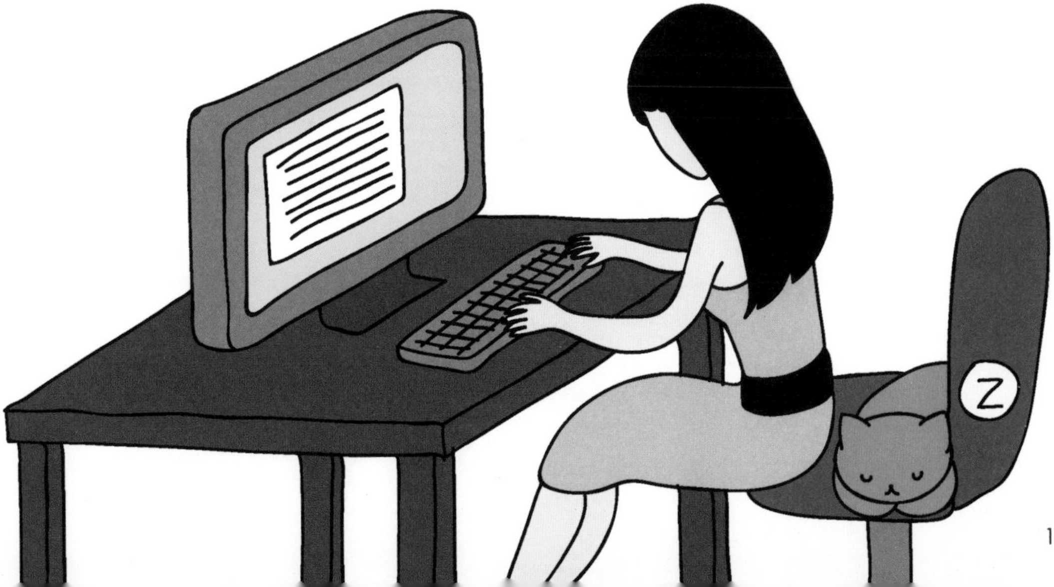
Z

Andrews McMeel Publishing
a division of Andrews McMeel Universal
1130 Walnut Street, Kansas City, Missouri 64106

www.andrewsmcmeel.com

18 19 20 21 22 SDB 10 9 8 7 6 5 4 3 2 1

ISBN: 978-1-4494-8943-4

Library of Congress Control Number: 2017952415

Editor: Patty Rice
Art Director: Diane Marsh
Production Editor: Dave Shaw
Production Manager: Tamara Haus

ATTENTION: SCHOOLS AND BUSINESSES
Andrews McMeel books are available at quantity
discounts with bulk purchase for educational, business,
or sales promotional use. For information, please
e-mail the Andrews McMeel Publishing Special Sales
Department: specialsales@amuniversal.com.